Y0-CDK-519

RESTful Java Web Services

Master core REST concepts and create RESTful web services in Java

Jose Sandoval

PUBLISHING

BIRMINGHAM - MUMBAI

RESTful Java Web Services

Copyright © 2009 Packt Publishing

All rights reserved. No part of this book may be reproduced, stored in a retrieval system, or transmitted in any form or by any means, without the prior written permission of the publisher, except in the case of brief quotations embedded in critical articles or reviews.

Every effort has been made in the preparation of this book to ensure the accuracy of the information presented. However, the information contained in this book is sold without warranty, either express or implied. Neither the author, nor Packt Publishing, and its dealers and distributors will be held liable for any damages caused or alleged to be caused directly or indirectly by this book.

Packt Publishing has endeavored to provide trademark information about all of the companies and products mentioned in this book by the appropriate use of capitals. However, Packt Publishing cannot guarantee the accuracy of this information.

First published: November 2009

Production Reference: 1051109

Published by Packt Publishing Ltd.
32 Lincoln Road
Olton
Birmingham, B27 6PA, UK

ISBN 978-1-847196-46-0

www.packtpub.com

Cover Image by Duraid Fatouhi (duraidfatouhi@yahoo.com)

Credits

Author
Jose Sandoval

Reviewers
Atanas Roussev

Richard Wallace

Acquisition Editor
Sarah Cullington

Development Editor
Dhiraj Chandiramani

Technical Editor
Ishita Dhabalia

Copy Editor
Sanchari Mukherjee

Indexer
Rekha Nair

Editorial Team Leader
Gagandeep Singh

Project Team Leader
Lata Basantani

Project Coordinator
Srimoyee Ghoshal

Proofreader
Lynda Silwoski

Graphics
Nilesh R. Mohite

Production Coordinator
Dolly Dasilva

Cover Work
Dolly Dasilva

About the Author

Jose Sandoval is a software developer based in Canada. He has played and worked with web technologies since the Mosaic web browser days. For the last 12 years he's worked or consulted for various financial institutions and software companies in North America, concentrating on large-scale Java web applications. He holds a Bachelor of Mathematics from the University of Waterloo and an MBA from Wilfrid Laurier University.

Aside from coding and writing, he enjoys watching a good soccer match and coaching his son's soccer team. You can learn more about his interests at his website www.josesandoval.com or his consulting firm's website www.sandoval.ca. Or you can reach him directly at jose@josesandoval.com.

I would like to thank Renee and Gabriel, for being the center and compass of my adventures; my family, for supporting me unconditionally; my friends and colleagues, for challenging me at every opportunity; my clients, for trusting me with their projects; and the entire Packt Publishing team, for helping me throughout the writing of this book.

About the Reviewers

Atanas Roussev is a father, an entrepreneur, and a software engineer. A certified Sun and Oracle developer, his work can be found at EA, Morgan Stanley, and many startups. His latest activities are in Java, GWT, mobile programming, and building HTTP4e (Eclipse add-on for HTTP and REST).

In the last decade he moved from Bulgaria to Vancouver, British Columbia, learning new words such as "timbits" and "double-double". He enjoys any offline time in the Rockies and he loves challenging his three kids at Guitar Hero and math.

You can find him at www.roussev.org or just e-mail him at atanas@roussev.org.

Richard Wallace is a software developer, currently working for Atlassian. He has been developing Java software for over seven years and has been a strong advocate for RESTful web services at Atlassian since starting there two years ago. He enjoys reading a good sci-fi book and spending time with his family.

> I'd like to thank my wonderful wife and kids for making life
> an exciting adventure everyday.

Table of Contents

Preface

If you're already familiar with REST theory, but are new to RESTful Java web services, and want to use the Java technology stack together with Java RESTful frameworks to create robust web services, this is the book for you.

This book is a guide for developing RESTful web services using Java and the most popular RESTful Java frameworks available today. This book covers the theory of REST, practical coding examples for RESTful clients, a practical outline of the RESTful design, and a complete implementation of a non-trivial web service using the frameworks Jersey's JAX-RS, Restlet's Lightweight REST, JBoss's JAX-RS RESTEasy, and Struts 2 with the REST plugin.

We cover each framework in detail so you can compare their strengths and weaknesses. This coverage will also provide you with enough knowledge to begin developing your own web services after the first reading. What's more, all the source code is included for you to study and modify. Finally, we discuss performance issues faced by web service developers and cover practical solutions for securing your web services.

What this book covers

Chapter 1, *RESTful Architectures*, introduces you to the REST software architectural style and discusses the constraints, main components, and abstractions that make a software system RESTful. It also elaborates on the details of HTTP requests and responses between clients and servers, and the use of RESTful web services in the context of Service-Oriented Architectures (SOA).

Chapter 2, *Accessing RESTful Services – Part 1*, teaches you to code four different RESTful Java clients that connect and consume RESTful web services, using the messaging API provided by Twitter.

Chapter 3, *Accessing RESTful Services – Part 2*, shows you how to develop a mashup application that uses RESTful web services that connect to Google, Yahoo!, Twitter, and TextWise's SemanticHacker API. It also covers in detail what it takes to consume JSON objects using JavaScript.

Chapter 4, *RESTful Web Services Design*, demonstrates how to design a micro-blogging web service (similar to Twitter), where users create accounts and then post entries. It also outlines a set of steps that can be used to design any software system that needs to be deployed as a RESTful web service.

Chapter 5, *Jersey: JAX-RS*, implements the micro-blogging web service specified in Chapter 4 using Jersey, the reference implementation of Sun's Java API for RESTful Web Services.

Chapter 6, *The Restlet Framework*, implements the micro-blogging web service specified in Chapter 4 using the Restlet framework, using two of its latest versions, 1.1 and 2.0.

Chapter 7, *RESTEasy: JAX-RS*, implements the micro-blogging web service specified in Chapter 4 using JBoss's RESTEasy framework.

Chapter 8, *Struts 2 and the REST Plugin*, implements the micro-blogging web service specified in Chapter 4 using Struts 2 framework (version 2.1.6) together with the REST plugin. This chapter covers configuration of Struts 2 and the REST plugin, mapping of URIs to Struts 2 action classes, and handling of HTTP requests using the REST plugin.

Chapter 9, *Restlet Clients and Servers*, extends coverage of the Restlet framework. This chapter looks at the client connector library and the standalone server library.

Chapter 10, *Security and Performance*, explores how to secure web services using HTTP Basic Authentication, and covers the OAuth authentication protocol. This chapter also covers the topics of availability and scalability and how they relate to implementing high performing web services.

What you need for this book

At the beginning of each chapter, you're given a list of the tools you will need to code and to compile the sample applications presented. However, the main software tools needed are the latest Java JDK and the latest Tomcat web server – these tools are available for any modern operating system.

Who this book is for

This book is for developers who want to code RESTful web services using the Java technology stack together with any of the frameworks Jersey's JAX-RS, Restlet's Lightweight REST, JBoss's JAX-RS RESTEasy, and Struts 2 with the REST plugin.

You don't need to know REST, as we cover the theory behind it all; however, you should be familiar with the Java language and have some understanding of Java web applications.

For each framework, we develop the same web service outlined in Chapter 4, *RESTful Web Services Design*. This is a practical guide and a greater part of the book is about coding RESTful web services, and not just about the theory of REST.

Conventions

In this book, you'll find a number of different styles of text that differentiate between sections in every chapter. Here are some examples of these styles, and an explanation of their meaning.

Code words in text are shown as follows (note the keyword `true`): "Without this directive set to `true`, our application will not identify resource classes to handle HTTP requests."

A block of code is set as follows:

```
if (acceptHeader == null || acceptHeader.isEmpty()
    || acceptHeader.equals("application/xml")) {
    representation = UserBO.getAllXML();
} else if (acceptHeader.equals("application/json")) {
    representation = UserBO.getAllJSON();
    type = "json";
}
```

When we wish to draw your attention to a particular portion of a code block, the relevant lines or items are set in bold as follows:

```
@GET
@Produces("application/xml")
public String getXML() {
return UserBO.getAllXML();
}
```

Any command-line input or output is written as follows:

```
javac -classpath "/apache-tomcat-6.0.16/lib/servlet-api.jar;commons-
logging-1.1.1.jar;commons-codec-1.3.jar;commons-httpclient-3.1.jar"
*.java
```

New terms and **important words** are shown in bold.

Words that you see on the screen in menus or dialog boxes appear in the text bolded, for example, "Note the **Response** in the right pane of the Swing application."

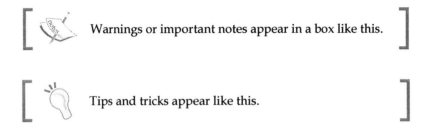

Warnings or important notes appear in a box like this.

Tips and tricks appear like this.

Reader feedback

Feedback from our readers is always welcomed. Let us know what you think about this book—what you liked or may have disliked. Reader feedback is important to us and helps us develop titles that offer you the most value for your money.

To send us general feedback, simply send an email to feedback@packtpub.com, mentioning the book's title in the subject of your message.

If there is a book that you need and would like to see us publish, please send us a note in the **SUGGEST A TITLE** form on www.packtpub.com or email suggest@packtpub.com.

If there is a topic that you have expertise in and are interested in writing a book about it or in contributing to one, see our author guide on www.packtpub.com/authors.

Customer support

Now that you are the proud owner of a Packt book, we have a number of things to help you to get the most from your purchase.

Downloading the example code for the book

Visit http://www.packtpub.com/files/code/6460_Code.zip.

Errata

Although we have taken every opportunity to ensure the accuracy of our content, mistakes do happen. If you find mistakes in one of our books—in the text or the code samples—we would be grateful if you report them to us. Reporting errors or inaccuracies will improve subsequent versions of this book.

If you find any errors, please report them by visiting http://www.packtpub.com/support, selecting the title of this book, clicking on the **let us know** link, and entering the details of the error in the provided form. Once your submission is verified, it will be added to the existing errata. Any existing errata can be viewed at http://www.packtpub.com/support.

Piracy

Piracy of copyrighted materials on the Internet is an ongoing problem across all media. At Packt, we take the protection of our copyrighted materials and licenses very seriously. If you come across any illegal copies of our works, in any form, on the Internet, please provide us with the website's address and name and we'll take immediate action. Please contact us at copyright@packtpub.com with a link to the suspected pirated material.

We appreciate your help in protecting our authors, and our ability to bring you valuable content.

Questions

You can contact us at questions@packtpub.com, if you are having a problem with any aspect of the book, and we will do our best to address it.

1
RESTful Architectures

In this chapter, we cover the REST software architectural style, as described in Roy Fielding's PhD dissertation. We discuss the set of constraints, the main components, and the abstractions that make a software system RESTful. We also look in detail at how data transfers take place between clients and servers. Finally, we look at how RESTful web services are used in the context of large **Service-Oriented Architectures (SOA)**.

This chapter distills the theory of REST to its main core. No previous knowledge about the subject is necessary, but I assume you are familiar with web technologies and the basics of the HTTP protocol.

What is REST?

The term **REST** comes from Roy Fielding's PhD dissertation, published in 2000, and it stands for **REpresentational State Transfer**. REST by itself is not an architecture; REST is a set of constraints that, when applied to the design of a system, creates a software architectural style. If we implement all the REST guidelines outlined in Fielding's work, we end up with a system that has specific roles for data, components, hyperlinks, communication protocols, and data consumers.

Fielding arrived at REST by evaluating all networking resources and technologies available for creating distributed applications. Without any constraints, anything and everything goes, leading us to develop applications that are hard to maintain and extend. With this in mind, he looks at document distributed application architectural styles beginning with what he calls the *null space* — which represents the availability of every technology and every style of application development with no rules or limits — and ends with the following constraints that define a RESTful system:

- It must be a client-server system
- It has to be stateless — there should be no need for the service to keep users' sessions; in other words, each request should be independent of others

- It has to support a caching system — the network infrastructure should support cache at different levels

- It has to be uniformly accessible — each resource must have a unique address and a valid point of access

- It has to be layered — it must support scalability

- It should provide code on demand — although this is an optional constraint, applications can be extendable at runtime by allowing the downloading of code on demand, for example, Java Applets

These constraints don't dictate what kind of technology to use; they only define how data is transferred between components and what are the benefits of following the guidelines. Therefore, a RESTful system can be implemented in any networking architecture available. More important, there is no need for us to invent new technologies or networking protocols: we can use existing networking infrastructures such as the Web to create RESTful architectures. Consequently, a RESTful architecture is one that is maintainable, extendable, and distributed.

Before all REST constraints were formalized, we already had a working example of a RESTful system: the Web. We can ask, then, why introduce these RESTful requirements to web application development when it's agreed that the Web is already RESTful.

We need to first qualify here what it's meant for the Web to be RESTful. On the one hand, the static web is RESTful, because static websites follow Fielding's definition of a RESTful architecture. For instance, the existing web infrastructure provides caching systems, stateless connection, and unique hyperlinks to resources, where resources are all of the documents available on every website and the representations of these documents are already set by files being browser readable (HTML files, for example). Therefore, the static web is a system built on the REST-like architectural style.

On the other hand, traditional dynamic web applications haven't always been RESTful, because they typically break some of the outlined constraints. For instance, most dynamic applications are not stateless, as servers require tracking users through container sessions or client-side cookie schemes. Therefore, we conclude that the dynamic web is not normally built on the REST-like architectural style.

We can now look at the abstractions that make a RESTful system, namely resources, representations, URIs, and the HTTP request types that make up the uniform interface used for client/server data transfers.

Resources

A RESTful resource is anything that is addressable over the Web. By addressable, we mean resources that can be accessed and transferred between clients and servers. Subsequently, a resource is a logical, temporal mapping to a concept in the problem domain for which we are implementing a solution.

These are some examples of REST resources:

- A news story
- The temperature in NY at 4:00 p.m. EST
- A tax return stored in IRS databases
- A list of code revisions history in a repository like SVN or CVS
- A student in some classroom in some school
- A search result for a particular item in a web index, such as Google

Even though a resource's mapping is unique, different requests for a resource can return the same underlying binary representation stored in the server. For example, let's say we have a resource within the context of a publishing system. Then, a request for "the latest revision published" and the request for "revision number 12" will at some point in time return the same representation of the resource: the last revision is revision 12. However, when the latest revision published is increased to version 13, a request to the latest revision will return version 13, and a request for revision 12 will continue returning version 12. As resources in a RESTful architecture, each of these resources can be accessed directly and independently, but different requests could point to the same data.

Because we are using HTTP to communicate, we can transfer any kind of information that can be passed between clients and servers. For example, if we request a text file from CNN, our browser receives a text file. If we request a Flash movie from YouTube, our browser receives a Flash movie. The data is streamed in both cases over TCP/IP and the browser knows how to interpret the binary streams because of the HTTP protocol response header *Content-Type*. Consequently, in a RESTful system, the representation of a resource depends on the caller's desired type (MIME type), which is specified within the communication protocol's request.

Representation

The representation of resources is what is sent back and forth between clients and servers. A representation is a temporal state of the actual data located in some storage device at the time of a request. In general terms, it's a binary stream together with its metadata that describes how the stream is to be consumed by either the client or the server (metadata can also contain extra information about the resource, for example, validation, encryption information, or extra code to be executed at runtime).

Throughout the life of a web service there may be a variety of clients requesting resources. Different clients are able to consume different representations of the same resource. Therefore, a representation can take various forms, such as an image, a text file, or an XML stream or a JSON stream, but has to be available through the same URI.

For human-generated requests through a web browser, a representation is typically in the form of an HTML page. For automated requests from other web services, readability is not as important and a more efficient representation can be used such as XML.

URI

A **Uniform Resource Identifier**, or **URI**, in a RESTful web service is a hyperlink to a resource, and it's the only means for clients and servers to exchange representations.

The set of RESTful constraints don't dictate that URIs must be hyperlinks. We only talk about RESTful URIs being hyperlinks, because we are using the Web to create web services. If we were using a different set of supporting technologies, a RESTful URI would look completely different. However, the core idea of addressability would still remain.

In a RESTful system, the URI is not meant to change over time, as the architecture's implementation is what manages the services, locates the resources, negotiates the representations, and then sends back responses with the requested resources. More important, if we were to change the structure of the storage device at the server level (swapping database servers, for example), our URIs will remain the same and be valid for as long the web service is online or the context of a resource is not changed.

Without REST constraints, resources are accessed by location: typical web addresses are fixed URIs. For instance, if we rename a file on a web server, the URI will be different; if we move a file to a different directory tree in a web server, the URI will change. Note that we could modify our web servers to execute redirects at runtime to maintain addressability, but if we were to do this for every file change, our rules would become unmanageable.

Uniform interfaces through HTTP requests

In previous sections, we introduced the concepts of resources and representations. We said that resources are mappings of actual entity states that are exchanged between clients and servers. Furthermore, we discussed that representations are negotiated between clients and servers through the communication protocol at runtime—through HTTP. In this section, we look in detail at what it means to exchange these representations, and what it means for clients and servers to take actions on these resources.

Developing RESTful web services is similar to what we've been doing up to this point with our web applications. However, the fundamental difference between modern and traditional web application development is how we think of the actions taken on our data abstractions. Specifically, modern development is rooted in the concept of nouns (exchange of resources); legacy development is rooted in the concept of verbs (remote actions taken on data). With the former, we are implementing a RESTful web service; with the latter, we are implementing an **RPC**-like service (**Remote Procedure Call**). What's more, a RESTful service modifies the state of the data through the representation of resources; an RPC service, on the other hand, hides the data representation and instead sends commands to modify the state of the data at the server level (we never know what the data looks like). Finally, in modern web application development we limit design and implementation ambiguity, because we have four specific actions that we can take upon resources—**Create**, **Retrieve**, **Update**, and **Delete** (**CRUD**). On the other hand, in traditional web application development, we can have countless actions with no naming or implementation standards.

Therefore, with the delineated roles for resources and representations, we can now map our CRUD actions to the HTTP methods POST, GET, PUT, and DELETE as follows:

Data action	HTTP protocol equivalent
CREATE	POST
RETRIEVE	GET
UPDATE	PUT
DELETE	DELETE

In their simplest form, RESTful web services are networked applications that manipulate the state of resources. In this context, resource manipulation means resource creation, retrieval, update, and deletion. However, RESTful web services are not limited to just these four basic data manipulation concepts. On the contrary, RESTful web services can execute logic at the server level, but remembering that every result must be a resource representation of the domain at hand.

> A uniform interface brings all the aforementioned abstractions into focus. Consequently, putting together all these concepts we can describe RESTful development with one short sentence: we use URIs to connect clients and servers to exchange resources in the form of representations.

Let's now look at the four HTTP request types in detail and see how each of them is used to exchange representations to modify the state of resources.

GET/RETRIEVE

The method GET is used to RETRIEVE resources.

Before digging into the actual mechanics of the HTTP GET request, first, we need to determine what a resource is in the context of our web service and what type of representation we're exchanging.

For the rest of this section, we'll use the artificial example of a web service handling students in some classroom, with a location of `http://restfuljava.com/`. For this service, we assume an XML representation of a student to look as follows:

```
<student>
    <name>Jane</name>
    <age>10</age>
    <link>/students/Jane</link>
</student>
```

And a list of students to look like:

```
<students>
    <student>
        <name>Jane</name>
        <age>10</age>
        <link>/students/Jane</link>
    </student>
    <student>
        <name>John</name>
        <age>11</age>
```

```
            <link>/students/John</link>
        </student>
        <link>/students</link>
    </students>
```

With our representations defined, we now assume URIs of the form
`http://restfuljava.com/students` to access a list of students, and
`http://restfuljava.com/students/{name}` to access a specific student that has
the unique identifier of value `name`.

We can now begin making requests to our web service. For instance,
if we wanted the record for a student with the name *Jane*, we make a request to the
URI `http://restfuljava.com/students/Jane`. A representation of `Jane`, at the
time of the request, may look like:

```
<student>
    <name>Jane</name>
    <age>10</age>
    <link>/students/Jane</link>
</student>
```

Subsequently, we can access a list of students through the URI
`http://restfuljava.com/students`. The response from the service
will contain the representation of all students and may look like (assuming there
are two students available):

```
<students>
    <student>
        <name>Jane</name>
        <age>10</age>
        <link>/students/Jane</link>
    </student>
    <student>
        <name>John</name>
        <age>11</age>
        <link>/students/John</link>
    </student>
    <link>/students</link>
</students>
```

Now let's have a look at the request details. A request to retrieve a `Jane` resource uses the `GET` method with the URI `http://restfuljava.com/students/Jane`. A sequence diagram of our `GET` request looks as follows:

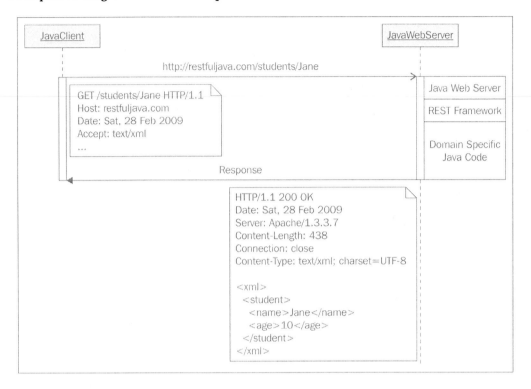

What's happening here?

1. A Java client makes an HTTP request with the method type `GET` and `Jane` as the identifier for the student.

2. The client sets the representation type it can handle through the *Accept* request header field.

3. The web server receives and interprets the GET request to be a retrieve action. At this point, the web server passes control to the RESTful framework to handle the request. Note that RESTful frameworks don't automatically retrieve resources, as that's not their job. The job of a framework is to ease the implementation of the REST constraints. Business logic and storage implementation is the role of the domain-specific Java code.

4. The server-side program looks for the Jane resource. Finding the resource could mean looking for it in a database, a filesystem, or a call to a different web service.

5. Once the program finds Jane, it converts the binary data of the resource to the client's requested representation.

6. With the representation converted to XML, the server sends back an HTTP response with a numeric code of 200 together with the XML representation as the payload. Note that if there are any errors, the HTTP server reports back the proper numeric code, but it's up to the client to correctly deal with the failure.

All the messages between client and server are standard HTTP protocol calls. For every retrieve action, we send a GET request and we get an HTTP response back with the payload of the response being the representation of the resource or, if there is a failure, a corresponding HTTP error code (for example, 404 if a resource is not found; 500, if there is a problem with the Java code in the form of an exception).

Getting a representation for all students works the same way as getting a representation for a single student, though we now use the URI http://restfuljava.com/students and the result is the XML representation:

```
<students>
    <student>
        <name>Jane</name>
        <age>10</age>
        <link>/students/Jane</link>
    </student>
    <student>
        <name>John</name>
        <age>11</age>
        <link>/students/John</link>
    </student>
    <link>/students</link>
</students>3
```

The HTTP GET method should only be used to retrieve representations. As we know, we can use a GET request to update the state of data in the server, but this is not recommended. A GET request must be safe and idempotent. (For more information, see http://www.w3.org/DesignIssues/Axioms.)

For a request to be safe, it means that multiple requests to the same resource don't change the state of the data in the server. Assume we have a representation R and requests happen at time t. Then, a request at time t1 for resource R returns R1; subsequently, a request at time t2 for resource R returns R2; provided that no further update actions have been taken between t1 and t2, then R1 = R2 = R.

For a request to be idempotent, it means that multiple calls to the same action don't change the state of the resource. For example, multiple calls to create a resource R at time t1, t2, and t3 means that R will exist only as R and that calls at times t2 and t3 are ignored.

POST/CREATE

The method POST is used to CREATE resources.

Because we are creating a student, we use the HTTP method POST. Again, the URI to create a new student in our list is http://restfuljava.com/students/Jane. The method type for the request is set by the client.

Assume Jane didn't exist in our list, and we want to add her. Our new Jane XML representation looks like:

```
<student>
    <name>Jane</name>
    <age>10</age>
    <link></link>
</student>
```

Note that the link element is part of the representation, but it's empty because this value is generated at runtime and not created by the client sending the POST request. This is just a convention for this example; however, clients using a web service can dictate the structure of URIs.

Now, the sequence diagram of our POST request looks as follows:

What's happening here?

1. A Java client makes a request to the URI `http://restfuljava.com/students/Jane`, with the HTTP method set to POST.

2. The POST request carries with it the payload in the form of an XML representation of `Jane`.

3. The server receives the request and lets the REST framework handle it; our code within the framework executes the proper commands to store the representation (again, the storage device could be anything).

4. Once storing of the new resource is completed, a response is sent back: if it's successful, we send a code of 200; if it's a failure, we send the appropriate error code.

PUT/UPDATE

The method PUT is used to UPDATE resources.

To update a resource, we first need its representation in the client; second, at the client level we update the resource with the new value(s) we want; and, finally, we update the resource using a PUT request together with the representation as its payload.

We're omitting the GET request to retrieve `Jane` from the web service, as it's the same one we illustrated in the previous section. We must, however, modify the representation at the client level first. Assume that we already have the student representation of `Jane` in the client and we want to change her age from 10 to 12. Our original student representation looks as follows:

```
<student>
    <name>Jane</name>
    <age>10</age>
    <link>/students/Jane</link>
</student>
```

Changing Jane's age to 12, our representation looks as follows:

```
<student>
    <name>Jane</name>
    <age>12</age>
    <link>/students/Jane</link>
</student>
```

We are now ready to connect to our web service to update `Jane` by sending the PUT request to `http://restfuljava.com/students/Jane`. The sequence diagram of our PUT request looks as follows:

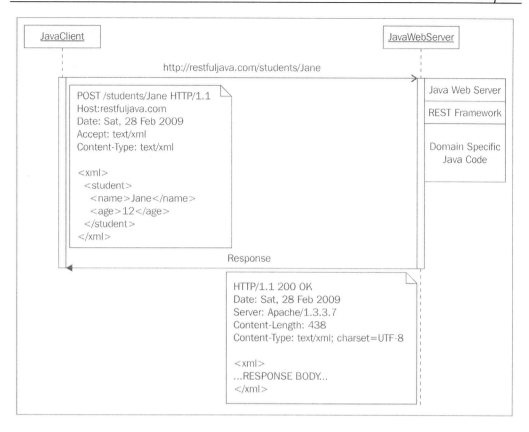

What's happening here?

1. A Java client makes a PUT request to `http://restfuljava.com/students/Jane`, with the new XML definition as its payload.

2. The server receives the request and lets the REST framework handle it. At this point, we let our code execute the proper commands to update the representation of `Jane`.

3. Once completed, a response is sent back.

DELETE/DELETE

The method DELETE is used to DELETE representations.

Finally, deleting a resource makes use of the same URI we've used in the other three cases.

Assume we want to delete `Jane` from our data storage. We send a DELETE request to our service with the URI `http://restfuljava.com/students/Jane`. The sequence diagram for our DELETE request looks like:

What's happening here?

1. A Java client makes a DELETE request to `http://restfuljava.com/students/Jane`.

2. The server receives the request and lets the REST framework handle it. At this point, our code executes the proper commands to delete the representation of `Jane`.

3. Once completed, a response is sent back.

And just like that, we've covered the main actions we can take with resources in a RESTful web service. We don't know what the client is doing with the representations, we don't know how the web service implements data storage, and we don't know what technology is used for the service. All we know is that we have a well behaved web service that adheres to the RESTful guidelines: our client and server communicate over HTTP, we use the communication protocol to send action requests, and our resource representations are sent back and forth through unchanging URIs.

 A note about our sequence diagrams: we're assuming that all the underlying technologies to be Java technologies (servers and clients). However, these are just components in the whole architecture and the explanations apply to any technology stack.

Web services and the big picture

As per the definition given by the World Wide WebConsortium (http://www.w3.org/), a web service is a computing system that exchanges XML messages with other systems using HTTP as the communication protocol. In addition, a web service is an independent computing unit that implements a single business requirement. The ultimate goal for web service developers, however, is to chain as many of them as possible to solve problems of increasing complexity. And because they are available over the Internet, they offer an attractive scalable computing architecture.

What kind of problem do web services solve?

There are two main areas where web services are used:

- Software companies opening their APIs to the public using web services
- Within large enterprises to support operations

First, web companies are beginning to open their doors to developers using publicly available APIs. Companies like Google, Yahoo!, Amazon, and Facebook are using web services to offer new products that rely on their massive hardware infrastructures. Google and Yahoo! offer their search services; Amazon offers its on-demand hosting storage infrastructure; and Facebook offers its platform for targeted marketing and advertising campaigns. With the help of web services, these companies have opened the door for the creation of products that didn't exist just five years ago.

Second, web services are being used within the enterprise to connect previously disjointed departments, such as marketing and manufacturing. The large enterprise is in fact more attractive to web service developers because of the internal controls of data distribution, potential cost savings, and minimized security concerns, as these large data systems are not open to the world (though, if they need to be open to the world outside, developers can control their security).

By connecting more than one department to share information using web services, we begin to enter the territory of the newly coined term **Service-Oriented Architecture**. Implementing an SOA inside an organization is not easy, as it encompasses not only IT departments but also higher circles of management. In other words, creating an SOA culture requires a large investment in IT and a strategic shift in operations.

To our advantage, we can integrate RESTful systems into a web service-oriented computing environment. What's more, we can fully use RESTful web services in the larger umbrella of SOA, as REST is not the system's architecture in itself, but it's a set of constraints that when applied to system design and implementation lead to a RESTful architecture. And because our definition of a web service doesn't dictate the implementation details of a computing unit, we can easily incorporate RESTful web services to solve large scale problems. Furthermore, with REST we have the added bonus of minimizing implementation, communication, and distribution complexity because we forgo XML-based services like SOAP/WSDL and we stick to using standard hardware and network technologies like XML and HTTP.

With this larger view of SOA, we begin to see how REST has the potential to impact new computing models being developed. Moreover, we can take advantage of RESTful frameworks freely available for the Java technology stack and begin implementing RESTful web services, which is the whole purpose of this book.

Summary

We have covered a lot of ground in this chapter. But we now have a better understanding of what REST represents and what it doesn't represent. For example, we know that REST is not a software architecture, but a set of constraints that, when applied to develop web services, creates a software architectural style, an architectural style that clearly delineates the roles of resources and representations and the way HTTP protocol is used to negotiate the appropriate representations that are exchanged as HTTP messages.

Finally, we covered why RESTful architectures are gaining track as the main distribution mode of web services not only for public APIs, but also within the Service Oriented Architectures used in large operations.

With the theory of REST out of the way, we are ready to begin using existing web services, designing custom RESTful web services, and, most importantly, implementing our own web services with the aid of existing RESTful frameworks and the Java technology stack. So, dust off your keyboard and let's begin developing RESTful Java Web Services.

2
Accessing RESTful Services — Part 1

The Java technology stack provides multiple client options, including command-line applications, desktop applications, and web applications. Our job in this chapter is to code all these client types as RESTful Java clients that connect and consume RESTful web services. The service we'll use for all our examples is the messaging API provided by Twitter (`http://www.twitter.com/`). Note that you don't have to have a Twitter account or know what Twitter is to take full advantage of all the code samples in this chapter.

Getting the tools

For this chapter, we need the latest Java JDK available—version 6 or later will work fine. Because we use the Jakarta Commons HTTPClient package, we also need the Commons Logging and Commons Codec packages. For our Swing application, we need the Swing Application Framework and the SwingWorker packages. Finally, we need the latest Tomcat web server—the JSP and Servlet code samples run on version 6.0 or later.

The following table lists the tools we need and where to get them (all freely available for download):

Software	Web location
Java JDK	`http://java.sun.com/`
Apache Tomcat	`http://tomcat.apache.org/download-60.cgi`
Jakarta Commons HTTPClient	`http://hc.apache.org/httpclient-3.x/`
Jakarta Commons Logging	`http://commons.apache.org/logging/`
Jakarta Commons Codec	`http://commons.apache.org/codec/`
Swing Application Framework	`https://appframework.dev.java.net/`
SwingWorker	`https://swingworker.dev.java.net/`

Download and install the Java JDK and Tomcat server, if you don't already have them in your machine. Also, download and unpack the rest of the JAR files in a handy location, for example, on your hard drive's root directory — the location of these files doesn't matter, as long as you know where they are at the time of compilation.

RESTful clients

A large part of our job when working with web services is consuming resource representations. Depending on the problem we are solving, we can choose from multiple client options. For example, a command-line application, a GUI Swing application, or a web application. For each client, we should know how to create reliable connections and how to handle the responses.

One of the strengths of the Java architecture is the abstraction of client/server connectivity over HTTP. Therefore, we'll use the standard `java.net` package provided with the latest JDK. Furthermore, we'll consume different representation types for each sample client in this chapter. For example, for the command-line application we display the result as it comes from the server, which is an XML formatted stream. With our JFC or Swing application, we will display the result in a more readable format and we'll create a reusable GUI testing client. Finally, for the JSP example we'll use RSS and the web browser to display the results.

Java command-line application

Connecting to a RESTful web service takes no more work than directly connecting to the service through an HTTP connection. For our first RESTful client, we'll use the command line to connect to Twitter's RESTful web service, which returns the last 20 public status updates.

Twitter is a micro-blogging platform that lets multiple users update their status using 140 characters at a time. Furthermore, users can follow each other by adding other users to their network of friends. Twitter stores these updates on its servers, and by default they are publicly available, which is why we are using it in our RESTful clients.

Our client code is listed as follows:

```java
import java.io.BufferedReader;
import java.io.IOException;
import java.io.InputStreamReader;
import java.net.MalformedURLException;
import java.net.URL;
import java.net.URLConnection;

public class RESTClient {
  public static void main(String[] args) {
    try {
      URL twitter = new URL("http://twitter.com/statuses
                                        /public_timeline.xml");
      URLConnection tc = twitter.openConnection();
      BufferedReader in = new BufferedReader(new InputStreamReader(
                                        tc.getInputStream()));
      String line;
      while ((line = in.readLine()) != null) {
        System.out.println(line);
      }
      in.close();
    } catch (MalformedURLException e) {
        e.printStackTrace();
      } catch (IOException e) {
          e.printStackTrace();
        }
    }
}
```

This is as simple as we can get, yet it's a fully-RESTful client. The first thing to note is the web service URI. The location for Twitter's API is `http://twitter.com/statuses/public_timeline.xml`. This is our resource's URI and points to the last 20 public status updates.

To connect to this web service, we first need to instantiate a `URL` object for the service's URI. Then, we open an `URLConnection` object for the Twitter URL instance. The method call to `twitter.openConnection()` executes an HTTP GET request. The lines that connect to the web service are as follows:

```
URL twitter = new URL("http://twitter.com/statuses
                                        /public_timeline.xml");
URLConnection tc = twitter.openConnection();
```

Once we have a connection established the server returns an HTTP response. The response's payload is an XML representation of the updates. For simplicity, we opt to dump the XML payload to the standard out stream, as follows:

```
BufferedReader in = new BufferedReader(new
                        InputStreamReader(tc.getInputStream()));
String line;
while ((line = in.readLine()) != null) {
     System.out.println(line);
}
```

First, we read the connection's response stream into a `BufferedReader` object. We then loop through each line of the stream, but first we assign it to a String object, which holds the value of each line in the stream. Subsequently, we display each line as it's read within the `while` loop with `System.out.println(line)`. Finally, we enclose all our code in a `try/catch` statement, and we send any exception messages to the standard out stream.

Before running the application, we need to compile it with the following command:

```
javac RESTClient.java
```

To run it, we use the command:

```
java RESTClient
```

This is the first Twitter public status update from an XML structure of 20:

```
<?xml version="1.0" encoding="UTF-8"?>
<statuses type="array">
   <status>
      <created_at>Mon Mar 23 23:39:06 +0000 2009</created_at>
      <id>1378638355</id>
      <text>Cricket: Dravid on the edge of history: As India secured
            their first test win on New Zealand soil in 33 years
```

```
                  an..... http://ff.im/-1GAcJ</text>
      <source>&lt;a
            href=&quot;http://friendfeed.com/&quot;&gt;
                  FriendFeed&lt;/a&gt;</source>
      <truncated>false</truncated>
      <in_reply_to_status_id />
      <in_reply_to_user_id />
      <favorited>false</favorited>
      <id>25268999</id>
      <name>all about cricket</name>
      <screen_name>allaboutcricket</screen_name>
      <description>Aggregator of Cricket News</description>
      <location></location>
      <profile_image_url>http://static.twitter.com/images
            /default_profile_normal.png</profile_image_url>
      <url>http://Don't have a site at the moment</url>
      <protected>false</protected>
      <followers_count>68</followers_count>
      </user>
      </status>
[19 more status elements removed]
      </statuses>
```

The above result only displays one status update to save space, but we get the idea: we connect to the web service, we get a response back. We won't go into the details of the XML structure, though they are found at `http://apiwiki.twitter.com/Twitter-API-Documentation`.

The API's documentation tells us that if we change the `.xml` extension we get different resource representations. Specifically, we can change `.xml` to `.json`, `.rss`, or `.atom`. For example, if we request the updates in a **JSON (JavaScript Object Notation)** format, the only change we need to make to our program above is in the following line:

```
URL twitter = new URL("http://twitter.com/statuses/
                                    public_timeline.json");
```

Again, to save space, we only show the first status update (you can get Twitter's JSON details from the API documentation):

```
[{"user":{"followers_count":62,"description":"","url":"ht
tp:\/\/www.facebook.com\/profile.php?id=1057301622","profile_
image_url":"http:\/\/s3.amazonaws.com\/twitter_production\/
profile_images\/61699483\/dorkgf5_normal.png","protected":false,
"location":"New Jersey","screen_name":"CeliaTesta","name":"Celi
a Testa","id":16691180},"text":"@micheleeeex Lolz I don't think
so. My family is all in South Jersey.","truncated":false,"favorit
ed":false,"in_reply_to_user_id":15497704,"created_at":"Mon Mar 23
```

```
23:55:43 +0000 2009","source":"<a href=\"http:\/\/help.twitter.
com\/index.php?pg=kb.page&id=75\">txt<\/a>","in_reply_to_status_
id":null,"id":1378718102},...19 more status updates removed...]
```

Even though Twitter refers to this service as a RESTful web service, at the time of this book's writing, this particular API is not fully RESTful, because of a design choice. If we look closer at the API documentation, we note that the request for a resource's representation type is part of the URI and not the HTTP *Accept* header.

Specifically, we have a GET request, but we don't have an HTTP *Accept* header that tells the service what type of response to send back (we covered this in detail in Chapter 1). The API returns a representation that depends on the URI itself, namely http://twitter.com/statuses/public_timeline.FORMAT, where FORMAT can be .xml, .json, .rss, or .atom. As we saw already, if we change the .xml part of the URI to .json we get a JSON representation instead of an XML representation. This is not a fully-RESTful web service, because it doesn't adhere to all the REST constraints stipulated by Fielding. Nevertheless, this detail doesn't change the usefulness of the API for our exploration of RESTful Java clients.

Jakarta Commons HTTP Client

For the most part, the java.net package provides enough functionality to connect to all HTTP based services. However, the Jakarta Commons HTTP Client libraries give us granular control and easier-to-use HTTP connection objects, especially when we want to build our own, all-purpose RESTful web services tools. Therefore, lets look at how we can code our own clients using this library.

The full listing for the program using the Jakarta Commons library looks as follows:

```java
import java.io.IOException;
import org.apache.commons.httpclient.HttpClient;
import org.apache.commons.httpclient.HttpException;
import org.apache.commons.httpclient.HttpStatus;
import org.apache.commons.httpclient.methods.GetMethod;
public class RESTWithHTTPClient {
    public static void main(String[] args) {
        HttpClient client = new HttpClient();
        GetMethod method = new
        GetMethod("http://twitter.com/statuses/public_timeline.xml");
        try {
            int statusCode = client.executeMethod(method);
            if (statusCode == HttpStatus.SC_OK) {
                System.out.println(new
                        String(method.getResponseBody()));
```

```
        }
    } catch (HttpException e) {
        e.printStackTrace();
    } catch (IOException e) {
        e.printStackTrace();
    } finally {
        method.releaseConnection();
    }
    }
}
```

The result for this program is the same as previous one (the XML structure). First, we instantiate an HTTP client with the following statement:

```
HttpClient client = new HttpClient();
```

With our client instantiated, we now proceed to create an HTTP GET method object with the following statement:

```
GetMethod method = new GetMethod("http://twitter.com/statuses/
                                        public_timeline.xml");
```

With the client and method instantiated, we now need to execute the request with:

```
int statusCode = client.executeMethod(method);
```

Note that with the Commons HTTP Client library, we have more control and can easily add error checking to our program. For example, we output the response to the standard out stream only if we get an HTTP 200 status code:

```
if (statusCode == HttpStatus.SC_OK) {
    System.out.println(new String(method.getResponseBody()));
}
```

Finally, we need to close our open connection with the statement:

```
method.releaseConnection();
```

The Commons HTTP Client library depends on two more Commons projects: Commons Codec and Commons Logging. Therefore, to compile this RESTful client, we need to include both JAR files to our classpath. Assuming our JAR files are in the same place where our Java file is located, we compile the program as follows:

```
javac -classpath "commons-logging-1.1.1.jar;commons-codec-
1.3.jar;commons-httpclient-3.1.jar" RESTWithHTTPClient.java
```

To run it, we use:

```
java -classpath "commons-logging-1.1.1.jar;commons-codec-1.3.jar;commons-
httpclient-3.1.jar" RESTWithHTTPClient
```

> When compiling this code (and subsequent code samples in this book) in a UNIX or Linux environment, replace the character ; with :. Furthermore, you may have new JAR libraries from the ones used at the time of this writing; therefore, you may have to modify the classpath values to reflect newer versions.

Java desktop application

In this section we develop a Java Swing desktop RESTful client. The completed application looks as follows:

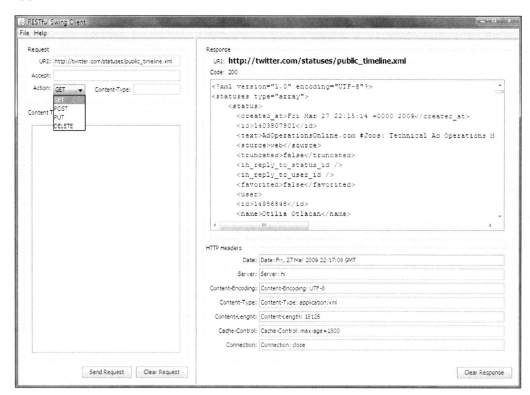

This application connects to any web service by using the value of the URI text field. Because RESTful web services are accessible through HTTP, we will use this application to test any of the web services we encounter, including the ones we code. The previous screenshot shows the request and result for our now familiar Twitter URI `http://twitter.com/statuses/public_timeline.xml`. In addition, when a request is sent to the URI, with any of the four request method types (GET, POST, PUT, or DELETE), the response is displayed on the right pane. We also display some of the HTTP response headers. Finally, we can clear either pane with its respective Clear Request or Clear Response buttons.

The code for this application is distributed among four files, with the following structure:

```
/RESTfulSwingClient/
            /RESTfulSwingClientApp.java
            /RESTfulSwingClientView.java
            /resources/
                    /RESTfulSwingClientApp.properties
                    /RESTfulSwingClientView.properties
```

The majority of the code creates the GUI client, and we include two Java properties files that provide display values to the GUI at runtime.

> We won't list the code for this program, but all the files are available for download from `http://www.packtpub.com/files/code/6460_Code.zip` (look for `Chapter2`)

We have two code portions of interest in the `RESTfulSwingClientView.java` file. First, we have the factory class that helps determine which type of request method to create. For each request method type, we need a concrete implementation that is used with the Commons HTTP client instance. The inner class looks as follows:

```java
class MethodFactory {
    public MethodFactory() {
        super();
    }

    public HttpMethod getMethod(String methodType, String URI)
            throws Exception {
        HttpMethod method = null;
        if (methodType.equals("GET")) {
            method =  new GetMethod(URI);
        } else if (methodType.equals("POST")) {
            method = new PostMethod(URI);
```

```
        } else if (methodType.equals("PUT")) {
            method = new PutMethod(URI);
        } else if (methodType.equals("DELETE")) {
            method = new DeleteMethod(URI);
        }

        if (method != null) {
            // If POST or PUT, we need "Content-Type"
            if (methodType.equals("POST") ||
                methodType.equals("PUT")) {
                ((EntityEnclosingMethod)
                 method).setRequestEntity(new
            StringRequestEntity(jTextAreaReqBody.getText().trim(),
            jTextFieldReqContentType.getText().trim(), "UTF-8"));
            }

            return method;
        }

        return null;
    }
}
```

This factory returns the appropriate `HttpMethod` object along with its payload, depending on the value of the drop-down field (as shown in the previous screenshot). For example, we need a GET, POST, PUT, or DELETE request method. Moreover, if we have a POST or PUT method request, we need the body in the `jTextAreaReqBody` component (the body is the name/value set of the request). So, we add the payload through:

```
((EntityEnclosingMethod) method).setRequestEntity(new
StringRequestEntity(jTextAreaReqBody.getText().trim(),
jTextFieldReqContentType.getText().trim(), "UTF-8"));
```

Finally, handling the send request uses similar code as we used in our Commons HTTP Client command-line application. The difference here is that we get the values from the GUI and then we update the view with the resulting values. The request handling code is part of this method in the same `RESTfulSwingClientView.java` file:

```
private void handleSendRequest() {
    String requestURI = jTextFieldReqURI.getText().trim();
    if (!requestURI.isEmpty()) {
        try {
            // Clear response
            handleClearResponse();

            // Instantiate client
            HttpClient client = new HttpClient();
```

```
        // Get method type from factory
        HttpMethod method = new
            MethodFactory().getMethod(jComboBoxMethod
            .getSelectedItem().toString(), requestURI);

        // Make http request
        int statusCode = client.executeMethod(method);

        // Update view
        jLabelURI.setText(requestURI);
        jLabelResultCode.setText("" + statusCode);
        jTextAreaResBody.setText(
            method.getResponseBodyAsString());

        // We omit the rest of the field updates here,
            but everything is part of the code listing...
    } catch (Exception ex) {
        ex.printStackTrace();
        // Let the user know something went wrong
        handleClearResponse();
        jLabelURI.setText("Error with URI: " + requestURI);
        jTextAreaResBody.setText(ex.getMessage());
    }
  }
}
```

If you have downloaded the code, you can compile the application with the following command (assuming you are inside the /RESTfulSwingClient/ directory and all JAR files are in the same location as the source code):

```
javac -classpath "commons-logging-1.1.1.jar;commons-codec-
1.3.jar;commons-httpclient-3.1.jar;appframework-1.0.3.jar;swing-worker-
1.1.jar" *.java
```

You run the application with the following command (note that the running *classpath* is different from the compiling *classpath*):

```
java -classpath "./;commons-logging-1.1.1.jar;commons-codec-
1.3.jar;commons-httpclient-3.1.jar;appframework-1.0.3.jar;swing-worker-
1.1.jar" RESTfulSwingClientApp
```

JSP application

For this section, we use the RSS representation of the last 20 status updates. The URI for the RSS feed is `http://twitter.com/statuses/public_timeline.rss`. We also use the web browser to display the RSS result—no need to create any viewing application. Using FireFox version 3.0 or later, the result of the request looks as follows:

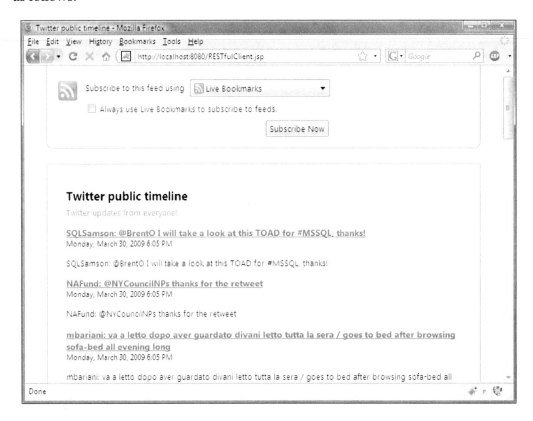

Since JSP is part of the standard JEE stack, we can use all the libraries and methods we have used to connect to any existing RESTful web service. To make the coding easier, we're not using the Commons HTTP Client. Instead, we use the same pattern we used in our first Java command RESTful client.

The full code listing to get the result in our screenshot looks as follows:

```
<%@ page contentType="text/xml; charset=UTF-8" %><%@ page
import="java.io.BufferedReader, java.io.IOException,
java.io.InputStreamReader, java.net.MalformedURLException,
java.net.URL, java.net.URLConnection" %><%
    // We removed CR and LF from the JSP code, because when the file
```

```
    // is generated on the server, it keeps those chars and makes the
       XML invalid (this is a JSP requirement)
    try {
        URL twitter = new
            URL("http://twitter.com/statuses/public_timeline.rss");
        URLConnection tc = twitter.openConnection();
        BufferedReader in = new BufferedReader(new
                InputStreamReader(tc.getInputStream()));
        String line;

        while ((line = in.readLine()) != null) {
         out.println(line);
        }

        in.close();
} catch (MalformedURLException e) {
        e.printStackTrace();
    } catch (IOException e) {
        e.printStackTrace();
    }
%>
```

We only have two new concepts in this listing. First, using the URI `http://twitter.com/statuses/public_timeline.rss` returns the latest public Twitter updates as an RSS feed (an RSS feed is a XML formatted file that is used by various syndicating programs and services; for details on RSS visit `http://www.rssboard.org/`). Second, we consume the response by writing it to the JSP standard out stream.

To run this code, we can create a file named `RESTfulClient.jsp` with the code listing above, and then we can copy or move the file into the `ROOT` directory of the webapps tree of the Tomcat install. We can now access the client with the URI `http://localhost:8080/RESTfulClient.jsp` (for this example, the JSP application is running on port 8080 of a Tomcat server).

By running this code we notice that the response of this JSP client is the same as if we were running the URI directly from Twitter's servers. We can think of this JSP client as a proxy for Twitter's API. Nevertheless, we can now connect to any web service available, manipulate the response as we please, and create our own web service mashups.

 A **mashup** is a web application that combines more than one web service.

Servlet application

Typically, we no longer code web applications that are fully dependent on Java Servlets. Gone are the days when we embedded HTML code within our Servlet response objects to render data and HTML at the same time. To display data and web GUI logic we now use a combination of JSP and Java technologies such as Java Beans and, possibly, web frameworks such as Struts or Spring for more complex applications.

We continue, however, to use Java Servlets to logically break down code that is not part of the GUI and is not part of the business layer. What's more, we can use Servlets to create simple, reusable programs to enhance the modularity of our applications. For example, we can use a Servlet to execute some portion of code and return an XML result, an image, or a calculation that is stateless and requires no more than a single request/response action.

For our sample application, we code a Java Servlet that connects to Twitter's web service to retrieve the XML representation of the public updates. We already have the code to do all the connections, so we only create a dynamic image out of the XML representation and display it as a part of an HTML page. This is not the most useful RESTful client, but it drives the point that we can create any type of application our business requirements dictate.

A run of the completed application looks as follows:

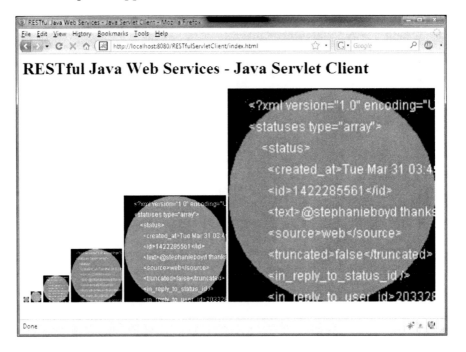

This HTML file calls our Servlet six times with the `<img src="/`
`RESTfulServletClient/servlet/RESTfulServletClient">` tag with different
`width` and `height` values.

Consequently, we can call the Servlet directly with the URI `http://localhost:8080/`
`RESTfulServletClient/servlet/RESTfulServletClient` and display the image by
itself, assuming that the web server is running on the 8080 port.

The direct call to our Java Servlet results in the following JPG rendering:

Let's now look at the code that creates these screenshots. First, we define our code
directory structure as follows:

/RESTfulServletClient/

> **/index.html**
>
> **/WEB-INF/**
>
> > **/web.xml**
> >
> > **/classes/**
> >
> > > **/RESTfulServletClient.java**

For this web application, we have three files. First, the `web.xml` file, which defines
our Java web application and looks as follows:

```
<?xml version="1.0" encoding="UTF-8"?>
<web-app version="2.5" xmlns="http://java.sun.com/xml/ns/javaee"
  xmlns:xsi="http://www.w3.org/2001/XMLSchema-instance"
  xsi:schemaLocation="http://java.sun.com/xml/ns/javaee
  http://java.sun.com/xml/ns/javaee/web-app_2_5.xsd">
  <servlet>
    <servlet-name>RESTfulServletClient</servlet-name>
```

```
    <servlet-class>RESTfulServletClient</servlet-class>
  </servlet>
  <servlet-mapping>
    <servlet-name>RESTfulServletClient</servlet-name>
    <url-pattern>/servlet/RESTfulServletClient</url-pattern>
  </servlet-mapping>
  <welcome-file-list>
    <welcome-file>index.html</welcome-file>
  </welcome-file-list>
</web-app>
```

Two things are happening here: on the one hand, we define a Servlet with the web server mapping; on the other hand, we tell the web application to treat the index.html as the welcome file within the context of the application.

Second, the index.html file looks as follows:

```
<html>
    <head>
        <title>RESTful Java Web Services - Java Servlet
        Client</title>
    </head>
    <body>
        <h1>RESTful Java Web Services - Java Servlet Client</h1>
        <img src="/RESTfulServletClient/servlet/RESTfulServletClient"
        width="10" height="10">
        <img src="/RESTfulServletClient/servlet/RESTfulServletClient"
        width="20" height="20">
        <img src="/RESTfulServletClient/servlet/RESTfulServletClient"
        width="50" height="50">
        <img src="/RESTfulServletClient/servlet/RESTfulServletClient"
        width="100" height="100">
        <img src="/RESTfulServletClient/servlet/RESTfulServletClient"
        width="200" height="200">
        <img src="/RESTfulServletClient/servlet/RESTfulServletClient"
        width="400" height="400">
    </body>
</html>
```

Note the call to our Servlet. We increase the values of the width and height attributes for each call. For instance, getting the image with width and height values of 10 looks as follows:

```
<img src="/RESTfulServletClient/servlet/RESTfulServletClient"
    width="10" height="10">
```

And third, the full listing for the Java Servlet file RESTfulServletClient.java looks as follows:

```java
import java.awt.Color;
import java.awt.Graphics;
import java.awt.image.BufferedImage;
import java.io.BufferedReader;
import java.io.IOException;
import java.io.InputStreamReader;
import java.net.URL;
import java.net.URLConnection;

import javax.imageio.ImageIO;
import javax.servlet.http.HttpServlet;
import javax.servlet.http.HttpServletRequest;
import javax.servlet.http.HttpServletResponse;
public class RESTfulServletClient extends HttpServlet {
    public void doGet(HttpServletRequest req,
                       HttpServletResponse res) {
        // Set mime-type
        res.setContentType("image/jpeg");
        BufferedReader in = null;
        try {
            // Create image
            BufferedImage bufferedImage = new BufferedImage(200, 200,
            BufferedImage.TYPE_INT_RGB);
            Graphics g = bufferedImage.getGraphics();

            // Change color and create a rectangle
            g.setColor(Color.gray);
            g.fillOval(0, 0, 200, 200);

            // Connect to Twitter API
            URL twitter = new
              URL("http://twitter.com/statuses/public_timeline.xml");
            URLConnection tc = twitter.openConnection();
            in = new BufferedReader(new
              InputStreamReader(tc.getInputStream()));
            String line;

            // Write each line in the rectangle.
            // Note that we are likely to have more lines than
               rectangle, but
            // it's OK
            int lineCount = 1;
            int yOffset = 20;
            g.setColor(Color.white);
            while ((line = in.readLine()) != null) {
                g.drawString(line, 20, lineCount * yOffset);
                lineCount++;
            }
```

```
        // Free graphic resources
        g.dispose();
        // Close in
        in.close();

        // Write the image as a jpg
        ImageIO.write(bufferedImage, "jpg",
            res.getOutputStream());
    } catch (IOException e) {
        e.printStackTrace();
    }
   }
  }
}
```

In this Servlet, we first instantiate a 2D Graphics object to which we can add components. Second, we connect to Twitter's API with the URI `http://twitter.com/statuses/public_timeline.xml`. Finally, we draw the XML on top of the oval and stream the image in our `HttpServletResponse` object.

We only need to compile the Servlet class, which is done using the following command (assuming we are in `/RESTfulServletClient/WEB-INF/classes/`):

**javac -classpath "/apache-tomcat-6.0.16/lib/servlet-api.jar"
RESTfulServletClient.java**

We are using all standard Java APIs, with the only new variable being the Servlet API. Since we didn't install the JEE version of the JDK, we can use Tomcat's `servlet-api.jar`, which is in the `/apache-tomcat-6.0.16/lib/` directory (assuming we have Tomcat installed in the root directory).

To run the application, we copy or move the `RESTfulServletClient` directory to the `/apache-tomcat-6.0.16/webapps/` directory, and then we restart Tomcat. With everything refreshed, we can access the URI `http://localhost:8080/RESTfulServletClient/` (we don't need the `index.html` in the URI, because in the file `web.xml` we told the web server to use `index.html` as the welcome file within the application's context).

Summary

We've coded and analyzed four different RESTful Java clients that connect to web services. However, sending XML representations to the standard out stream is not as exciting as creating new services with the representations of other services. With this in mind, we can use what we've learned in this chapter and continue exploring the possibility of combining two more web services to create our own mashups.

3
Accessing RESTful Services — Part 2

In this chapter, we develop a mashup application that uses freely-available RESTful web services. Our application connects to Google, Yahoo!, Twitter, and TextWise's SemanticHacker API. We make extensive use of Ajax calls and we study in detail how to consume JSON objects. The main technologies we use for the sample application are HTML, Java Servlets, JavaScript, and Prototype's Ajax library.

Getting the tools

The only new software we need to download for this chapter is the Prototype JavaScript library, assuming we have all the tools already installed from Chapter 2, *Accessing RESTful Services – Part 1.*

Prototype is available at `http://www.prototypejs.org/download`.

Each of the APIs we use are available through URIs, so we'll need an Internet connection to be available to run the full application.

Semantic search mashup

In Chapter 2, we looked at how to connect to and consume RESTful web services that use XML or JSON resource representations. In this chapter, we extend the concept to create an application that connects to multiple APIs to solve a single problem.

We develop a semantic blog. By semantic blog we mean that our application accepts blog entries and helps us to automatically search the Internet for the topic or topics we are blogging about. The application searches for relevant information in Google, Yahoo, and Twitter. We can, of course, go to each site to search manually for what we have in mind while writing the blog entry; however, we have tools (such as TextWise's API) that can semantically parse entire bodies of text.

The finished application we develop looks as follows:

The application does the following:

- When the **Title** field loses focus, we search Yahoo for the value in the field. The bottom panel on the left side displays the images found, and the top panel on the right side displays the web results.

- The action of the **Parse Entry** button sends the value of the **Entry** field to be analyzed by the semantic parsing API. The response from this service returns a snippet of HTML that is displayed in the **Tag Cloud** panel (middle left). Finally, we search Google and Twitter for the top value of the tag cloud and display the results in each panel on the right (middle for Google and bottom for Twitter).

- The action for the **Clear** button clears all the HTML elements for new input and output.

For this screenshot, we have searched for the term **java** for both the **Title** and the **Entry** fields.

Application architecture

Our blog runs as a web application and uses multiple Ajax calls to connect to a proxy Servlet layer, which then connects to multiple freely-available web services. The architecture of the application looks as follows:

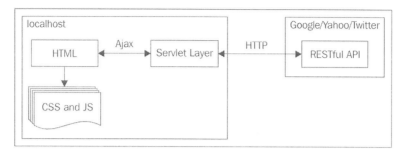

We've already covered all but one of the technologies used in this diagram, namely, the Ajax calls for which we use Prototype's Ajax library. Furthermore, we run the entire application from one HTML page and we consume all the resource representations as JSON objects at the UI layer with the help of JavaScript.

The code directory structure for our web application looks as follows:

```
/RESTfulMashupSearch/
                /index.html
                /prototype.js
                /style.css
                /WEB-INF/
                        /web.xml
                        /classes/
                                /MyGoogleSearch.java
                                /MySemanticParse.java
                                /MyTwitterSearch.java
                                /MyYahooImageSearch.java
                                /MyYahooSearch.java
                        /lib/
                                /commons-codec-1.3.jar
                                /commons-httpclient-3.1.jar
                                /commons-logging-1.1.1.jar
```

Everything presented here, including code listing, is a complete application. We include every line of code embedded in this chapter; however, if you don't want to code the application from scratch, but still want to follow along with a running local version, the code is available at `http://www.packtpub.com/files/code/6460_Code.zip` (look for `Chapter3`).

Web application definition

Let's begin with the web server layer. This application runs on any Java web server, but we'll assume Tomcat as we already have it installed from our coding samples in Chapter 2. The web application definition is part of the `web.xml` file and looks as follows:

```xml
<?xml version="1.0" encoding="UTF-8"?>
<web-app version="2.5"
    xmlns="http://java.sun.com/xml/ns/javaee"
    xmlns:xsi="http://www.w3.org/2001/XMLSchema-instance"
    xsi:schemaLocation="http://java.sun.com/xml/ns/javaee
    http://java.sun.com/xml/ns/javaee/web-app_2_5.xsd">
    <!-- Semantic Parser -->
    <servlet>
        <description>Parse entry and get cloud tag.</description>
        <display-name>MySemanticParse</display-name>
        <servlet-name>MySemanticParse</servlet-name>
        <servlet-class>MySemanticParse</servlet-class>
    </servlet>

    <servlet-mapping>
        <servlet-name>MySemanticParse</servlet-name>
        <url-pattern>/servlet/MySemanticParse</url-pattern>
    </servlet-mapping>
    <!-- Search Twitter -->
    <servlet>
        <description>Search Twitter.</description>
        <display-name>MyTwitterSearch</display-name>
        <servlet-name>MyTwitterSearch</servlet-name>
        <servlet-class>MyTwitterSearch</servlet-class>
    </servlet>

    <servlet-mapping>
        <servlet-name>MyTwitterSearch</servlet-name>
        <url-pattern>/servlet/MyTwitterSearch</url-pattern>
    </servlet-mapping>
```

```xml
<!-- Search Yahoo -->
<servlet>
    <description>Search Yahoo.</description>
    <display-name>MyYahooSearch</display-name>
    <servlet-name>MyYahooSearch</servlet-name>
    <servlet-class>MyYahooSearch</servlet-class>
</servlet>

<servlet-mapping>
    <servlet-name>MyYahooSearch</servlet-name>
    <url-pattern>/servlet/MyYahooSearch</url-pattern>
</servlet-mapping>

<!-- Search Yahoo Images -->
<servlet>
    <description>Search Yahoo Images.</description>
    <display-name>MyYahooImageSearch</display-name>
    <servlet-name>MyYahooImageSearch</servlet-name>
    <servlet-class>MyYahooImageSearch</servlet-class>
</servlet>

<servlet-mapping>
    <servlet-name>MyYahooImageSearch</servlet-name>
    <url-pattern>/servlet/MyYahooImageSearch</url-pattern>
</servlet-mapping>

<!-- Search Google -->
<servlet>
    <description>Search Google.</description>
    <display-name>MyGoogleSearch</display-name>
    <servlet-name>MyGoogleSearch</servlet-name>
    <servlet-class>MyGoogleSearch</servlet-class>
</servlet>

<servlet-mapping>
    <servlet-name>MyGoogleSearch</servlet-name>
    <url-pattern>/servlet/MyGoogleSearch</url-pattern>
</servlet-mapping>

<welcome-file-list>
    <welcome-file>index.html</welcome-file>
</welcome-file-list>
</web-app>
```

This is a typical Java web application definition file and declares the five Servlets we need. For example, assuming our web server is running in our local machine at `localhost` and port `8080`, we can make an HTTP requests to `http://localhost:8080/RESTfulMashupSearch/servlet/MyYahooSearch?query=US`.

User interface layer

Next, we have the user interface or view layer of our application. The HTML code includes a set of styles that takes care of the look and feel. The styles are defined in the style.css file, which looks as follows (the CSS file is also part of the downloadable package):

```
semanticJournal {
    width: 440px;
    float: left;
    padding-top: 0px;
    padding-left: 0px;
    padding-right: 16px;
    padding-bottom: 0px;
}

mainResult {
    width: 580px;
    float: left;
    padding-top: 0px;
    padding-left: 8px;
    padding-right: 0px;
    padding-bottom: 0px;
}

googleResult {
    width: 580px;
    height: 140px;
    float: left;
    overflow: auto;
    padding: 4px;
    margin: 2px;
    background: #E0FFC1;
    border-style: solid;
    border-color: #CFCFCF;
    border-width: 1px;
}

yahooResult {
    width: 580px;
    height: 140px;
    float: left;
    overflow: auto;
    padding: 4px;
    margin: 2px;
    margin: 2px;
    background: #FFD9D9;
```

```
        border-style: solid;
        border-color: #CFCFCF;
        border-width: 1px;
    }
    twitterResult {
        width: 580px;
        height: 140px;
        float: left;
        overflow: auto;
        padding: 4px;
        margin: 2px;
        background: #FFFFB9;
        border-style: solid;
        border-color: #CFCFCF;
        border-width: 1px;
    }

    formTextField {
        font-family: Arial, sans-serif;
        font-size: 12px;
        width: 440px;
    }

    formTextArea {
        font-family: Arial, sans-serif;
        font-size: 12px;
        width: 440px;
    }

    content {
        font-family: Arial, sans-serif;
        font-size: 12px;
    }

    cloud {
        width: 440px;
        float: left;
        padding: 4px;
        background: #EFEFEF;
        font-family: Arial, sans-serif;
        font-size: 12px;
        color: black;
        border-style: solid;
        border-color: #CFCFCF;
        border-width: 1px;
    }
```

```
imageResult {
    width: 440px;
    height: 200px;
    overflow: auto;
    float: left;
    padding: 4px;
    background: #CCCCCC;
    font-family: Arial, sans-serif;
    font-size: 12px;
    border-style: solid;
    border-color: #CFCFCF;
    border-width: 1px;
}
```

And the full listing for the `index.html` file looks as follows (note that the JavaScript functions are embedded in the HTML file for this example, but for a real application we recommend taking them out into their own JavaScript file and then including it as source):

```
<html>
 <head>
  <title>
    RESTful Java Web Services - RESTful Mashup Search
  </title>
  <link href="style.css" rel="stylesheet" type="text/css">

  <script type="text/javascript"
          src="prototype.js">
  </script>

  <script type="text/javascript">
  // Ajax call functions
  function doClear() {
    // Clear form
    document.searchForm.title.value = "";
    document.searchForm.entry.value = "";

    // Clear result pannels
    document.getElementById("myCloudResult").innerHTML = " ";
    document.getElementById("myYahooResult").innerHTML = "";
    document.getElementById("myGoogleResult").innerHTML = "";
    document.getElementById("myTwitterResult").innerHTML = "";
    document.getElementById("myImageResult").innerHTML = "";
  }

  function doSemanticParse() {
    // Validate input first
```

```
  if (document.searchForm.entry.value == "") {
    alert("Entry can't be empty.");
    return;
  }

  // Clear result pannels
  document.getElementById("myGoogleResult").innerHTML = "";
  document.getElementById("myTwitterResult").innerHTML = "";

  // Semantic parse
  var entry = escape(document.searchForm.entry.value);
  var params = "entry="  + entry;
  new Ajax.Updater(myCloudResult,
    '/RESTfulMashupSearch/servlet/MySemanticParse',
    {method: 'post', parameters: params, asynchronous:false});


  // Note that MySemanticParse sets a value in the session
  // for these services to search for the top cloud value
  doGoogleSearch();
  doTwitterSearch();
}

function handleOnTitleBlur() {
  var title = escape(document.searchForm.title.value);
  if (title != "") {
    doYahooSearch(title);
    doYahooImageSearch(title);
  }
}

function doGoogleSearch() {
  // We don't pass any parameters because the top cloud is set in
  // the HttpSession object
  new Ajax.Request('/RESTfulMashupSearch/servlet/MyGoogleSearch', {
    method: 'get',
    onSuccess: function(transport) {
      // eval() is used to parse the response
      var googleObject = eval('(' + transport.responseText + ')');

      // Update panel: only display 3 results
      var html = "<a href="
        + googleObject.responseData.results[0].unescapedUrl
        + " target=_gSearch>"
        + googleObject.responseData.results[0].titleNoFormatting
        + "</a><br/>"
        + googleObject.responseData.results[0].content
        + "<hr size=1 noshade color=#CFCFCF>";
```

```
      html = html + "<a href="
        + googleObject.responseData.results[1].unescapedUrl
        + " target=_gSearch>"
        + googleObject.responseData.results[1].titleNoFormatting
        + "</a><br/>"
        + googleObject.responseData.results[1].content
        + "<hr size=1 noshade color=#CFCFCF>";
      html = html + "<a href="
        + googleObject.responseData.results[2].unescapedUrl
        + " target=_gSearch>"
        + googleObject.responseData.results[2].titleNoFormatting
        + "</a><br/>"
        + googleObject.responseData.results[2].content;

      document.getElementById("myGoogleResult").innerHTML = html;
    }
  });
}

function doYahooSearch(value) {
  // Clear result pannel
  document.getElementById("myYahooResult").innerHTML = "";

  // Search
  new Ajax.Request('/RESTfulMashupSearch/servlet/MyYahooSearch
                                                    ?query='
    + value, {
    method: 'get',
    onSuccess: function(transport) {
      var yahooObject = eval('(' + transport.responseText + ')');

  // Update panel: only display 3 results
  var html = "<a href="
    + yahooObject.ResultSet.Result[0].Url
    + " target=_yahoo>" + yahooObject.ResultSet.Result[0].Title
    + "</a><br/>" + yahooObject.ResultSet.Result[0].Summary
    + "<hr size=1 noshade color=#CFCFCF>";
  html = html + "<a href=" + yahooObject.ResultSet.Result[1].Url
    + " target=_yahoo>" + yahooObject.ResultSet.Result[1].Title
    + "</a><br/>" + yahooObject.ResultSet.Result[1].Summary
    + "<hr size=1 noshade color=#CFCFCF>";
  html = html + "<a href="
    + yahooObject.ResultSet.Result[2].Url
    + " target=_yaoo>" + yahooObject.ResultSet.Result[2].Title
    + "</a><br/>" + yahooObject.ResultSet.Result[2].Summary;

  document.getElementById("myYahooResult").innerHTML = html;
    }
  });
```

```
}
function doYahooImageSearch(value) {
  // Clear result pannel
  document.getElementById("myImageResult").innerHTML = "";

  // Search
  new Ajax.Request
    ('/RESTfulMashupSearch/servlet/MyYahooImageSearch?query='
      + value, {
    method: 'get',
    onSuccess: function(transport) {
      var yahooObject = eval('(' + transport.responseText + ')');

      // Update panel: display 10 images
      var html = "";
      for (i = 0; i<10; i++) {
        html = html + "<a href="
          + yahooObject.ResultSet.Result[i].Url
          + " target=_yahoo><img src="
          + yahooObject.ResultSet.Result[i].Thumbnail.Url
          + "></a>";
      }

      document.getElementById("myImageResult").innerHTML = html;
    }
  });
}
function doTwitterSearch() {
  new Ajax.Request('/RESTfulMashupSearch/servlet/MyTwitterSearch', {
    method: 'get',
    onSuccess: function(transport) {
      var twitterObject = eval('(' + transport.responseText + ')');

      // Update panel: only display 3 results
      var html = "<a href=http://twitter.com/"
        + twitterObject.results[0].from_user + " target=_twitter>"
        + twitterObject.results[0].from_user + "</a>: "
        + twitterObject.results[0].text
        + "<hr size=1 noshade color=#CFCFCF>";
      html = html + "<a href=http://twitter.com/"
        + twitterObject.results[1].from_user
        + " target=_twitter>" + twitterObject.results[1].from_user
        + "</a>: " + twitterObject.results[1].text
        + "<hr size=1 noshade color=#CFCFCF>";
```

```
        html = html + "<a href=http://twitter.com/"
          + twitterObject.results[2].from_user
          + " target=_twitter>" + twitterObject.results[2].from_user
          + "</a>: " +  twitterObject.results[2].text;

        document.getElementById("myTwitterResult").innerHTML = html;
      }
    });
  }
  </script>
</head>
<body class="content">
 <div class="semanticJournal">
   <h1>RESTful Mashup: Semantic Search</h1>

   <table border="0" cellpadding="4" cellspacing="0" width="440"
         class="content">
     <form name="searchForm" method="GET">
       <tr><td>
         <b>Title</b><br />
         <input type="text" name="title" class="formTextField"
               onBlur="handleOnTitleBlur(); return false;">
       </td></tr>
       <tr><td width="80%">
         <b>Entry</b><br />
         <textarea name="entry"
                   class="formTextArea"
                   rows="4">
         </textarea>
       </td></tr>
       <tr><td align="right">
         <input type="button"
               value="Parse Entry"
               onClick="doSemanticParse();">
         <input type="button"
               value="Clear"
               onClick="doClear()">
       </td></tr>
     </form>
   </table>

   <br />
```

```
    <b>Tag Cloud (links open delicious.com bookmarks)</b>
    <div class="cloud">
      <div id="myCloudResult"> </div>
    </div>

    <p> </p>
    <b>Image search for top <cite>cloud</cite> tag.</b>
    <div class="imageResult">
      <div id="myImageResult"></div>
    </div>

  </div> <!-- semanticJournal div -->
  <div class="mainResult">
    <b>Yahoo search for <cite>Title</cite></b><br/>
    <div class="yahooResult">
      <div id="myYahooResult"></div>
    </div>

    <p> </p>
    <b>Google search for top <cite>cloud</cite> tag.</b><br/>
    <div class="googleResult">
      <div id="myGoogleResult"></div>
    </div>

    <p> </p>
    <b>Twitter search for top <cite>cloud</cite> tag.</b>
    <div class="twitterResult">
      <div id="myTwitterResult"></div>
    </div>

  </div> <!-- mainResult div -->
 </body>
</html>
```

As we said earlier, we're using Prototype's library and we include it as follows:

```
<script type="text/javascript" src="prototype.js"></script>
```

With the library included we can now explain the code that interacts with all the web services we're using. Within our HTML file we have defined the following seven JavaScript functions:

Function	Functionality
doClear()	As per our HTML and CSS code, we have declared div elements with their respective identifiers that we clear to display new information. We clear the elements by updating them in the DOM with an empty innerHTML value.
doSemanticParse()	In this function, we send the entry's value to our semantic API through an Ajax call. We use Prototype's Ajax.Updater() as follows:

```
new Ajax.Updater(myCloudResult,
'/RESTfulMashupSearch/servlet/
MySemanticParse', {method:
'post', parameters: params,
asynchronous:false});
```

The Ajax.Updater() function takes multiple parameters, but we only need three:

(1) The element in the DOM we need to update with the HTTP response.

(2) The URI that handles the request.

(3) A set of parameters that are needed with the URI, for example, we use the method POST and we pass as parameter the value of our textarea field. Finally, we tell the Ajax call to execute synchronously, because we set a value in the HttpSession that will be used by subsequent Servlet calls (this prevents simultaneous HTTP requests from our other Ajax calls, but it's not recommended for production applications).

The response object of the MySemanticParse Servlet is a cloud tag, and is already HTML formatted. What's more, the links in the tag point to delicious.com bookmarks. Therefore, we display the response as returned.

For more information about Prototype's Ajax library, see http://www.prototypejs.org/api/ajax/ and for more information about delicious's cloud tags see http://delicious.com/help/tagrolls.

Function	Functionality
`handleOnTitleBlur()`	We search Yahoo's web and image services for the title of the entry, by calling `doYahooSearch()` and `doYahooImageSearch()`. Both actions happen when the `title` form element loses focus.
`doGoogleSearch()`	This function uses another of Prototype's Ajax calls. For this case, we use the `Ajax.Request()` call. This function is different from `Ajax.Updater()`, as we manually handle the result with custom code for responses and DOM updates. Compare this with an `Ajax.Updater()` call where we pass the parameter of the element we want updated in the DOM.
	Handling of the response is done using the `onSuccess` function. The Servlet returns a JSON object, and the JSON object is stored in the variable `transport.responseText`, which is the response stream.
	Finally, we update the DOM object with the line: `document.getElementById("myGoogleResult").innerHTML = html;`
`doYahooSearch(value)`	Similar to the `doGoogleSearch()` function, we use the `Ajax.Request()` call. This function, however, uses the value of the `title` form element. And the response from our Servlet is the JSON representation of the search results.
	See Yahoo's search API for reference on the JSON object format: `http://developer.yahoo.com/search/web/V1/webSearch.html`.
`doYahooImageSearch(value)`	This is a similar call to Yahoo's search service, but the URI is different, as we're searching for images and not for web content.
	Note that we could save some lines of code by grouping the web and image searches; however, we create a Servlet for each service call to fully illustrate the process.
`doTwitterSearch()`	This function call performs a Twitter search using the `Ajax.Reqest()` call, and the JSON result is parsed accordingly.

Every Ajax call inside our functions follows the same pattern: first, we connect to our proxy Servlets to make the necessary request for our representations; and, second, we set the necessary API keys if needed, and we connect to the APIs to return the resource representations to the consuming client. Consuming the representations means parsing the JSON objects and displaying values as necessary.

Parsing JSON structures

Because we are using a web browser as our client, we use JSON for the format of all the resource representations requested—JSON is plain text over HTTP and can be manipulated easily with JavaScript.

The grammar for JSON objects is simple and requires the grouping of data definition and data values. First, elements are enclosed with curly brackets: { and }; second, values of elements come in pairs, have the structure of `"name":"value"`, and are comma separated; and, third, arrays are enclosed with square brackets: [and]. That's all there is to it. (For the full JSON grammar description, see `http://www.json.org/fatfree.html`.)

With our grouping definition explained, we can now combine multiple sets to create any kind of structure required. For example, a JSON result with multiple attributes and an array of multiple attributes could look as follows:

```
{some_name:{name:value, ..., name:value, some_name:[{name:value, ...,
name:value}, ..., {name:value, ..., name:value}]}}.
```

Before displaying any of the values in a JSON response, we need to convert it into a structure that we're familiar with—for instance, we know how to work with JavaScript object hierarchies.

To convert a JSON string into usable code we use the native JavaScript function `eval()`. In the case of a JSON stream, `eval()` transforms the stream into an object together with properties that are accessible without doing any string manipulation.

> JSON streams are snippets of JavaScript code and must be evaluated using the function `eval()` before we can use them as runtime objects. In general, executing JavaScript through `eval()` from untrusted sources opens applications to security risks because the value of the function's parameter is executed as JavaScript. However, for this application we trust that the JavaScript sent from each Servlet is a safe JSON structure.

Because an evaluated JSON object is similar to a DOM object, we traverse the tree using the dot or . character. Just as when traversing the DOM of an HTML page with `document.getElementById("SOME_ID")`, we can similarly traverse a JSON result. For example, a root element named `Root` with a sub element name `Element` can be accessed with `Root.Element`.

In the case of a Yahoo search request for the string "java" we get the following representation (this is only one record, but the response returns more than one):

```
{"ResultSet":{"type":"web","totalResultsAvailable":848000000,"to
talResultsReturned":10,"firstResultPosition":1,"moreSearch":"\/
WebSearchService\/V1\/webSearch?query=java&amp;appid=YahooDemo&
amp;region=us","Result":[{"Title":"Java.com","Summary":"Official
Java site from Sun. Includes Java software download,
information for developers, and examples of Java technology in
action.","Url":"http:\/\/www.java.com\/","ClickUrl":"http:\/\/www.
java.com\/","DisplayUrl":"www.java.com\/","ModificationDate":123960
6000,"MimeType":"text\/html","Cache":{"Url":"http:\/\/uk.wrs.yahoo.
com\/_ylt=A0S0mmCn4uRJZEsBtB_dmMwF;_ylu=X3oDMTBwZTdwbWtkBGNvbG8DZQ
Rwb3MDMQRzZWMDc3IEdnRpZAM-\/SIG=15a2ad56t\/EXP=1239823399\/**http%
3A\/\/74.6.239.67\/search\/cache%3Fei=UTF-8%26output=json%26appid=Ya
hooDemo%26query=java%26u=www.java.com\/%26w=java%26d=FYta4ExISoA9%26i
cp=1%26.intl=us","Size":"8862"}},...]}}
```

This looks like gibberish, but once we use `eval()` on this string we can then access the elements of the structure with our familiar object referencing. For example, if we want to know how many results are available, we access the value with `ResultSet.totalResultsAvailable` (this is the second name/value pair after the `ResultSet` instance). And if we want to access the `Title` value on the first `Result` element, we get it with `ResultSet.Result[0].Title` (this element is part of an array and elements are zero indexed).

If we go back to the JavaScript functions in our HTML file, we can clearly see how we parse the result and update the respective elements in the DOM. In the case of the `doYahooSearch()` function, we make a call to our proxy Servlet, then we consume the result and update the UI with the following code (we assume the `Result` array has up to three records returned; for some searched terms, however, this will not be the case and we may get a JavaScript error):

```
// Search
new Ajax.Request('/RESTfulMashupSearch/servlet/MyYahooSearch?query='
    + value, {
        method: 'get',
        onSuccess: function(transport) {
          var yahooObject = eval('(' + transport.responseText + ')');

          // Update panel: only display 3 results
          var html = "<a href=" + yahooObject.ResultSet.Result[0].Url
            + " target=_yahoo>"
            + yahooObject.ResultSet.Result[0].Title
            + "</a><br/>" + yahooObject.ResultSet.Result[0].Summary
            + "<hr size=1 noshade color=#CFCFCF>";
```

```
                    html = html + "<a href="
                      + yahooObject.ResultSet.Result[1].Url
                      + " target=_yahoo>"
                      + yahooObject.ResultSet.Result[1].Title
                      + "</a><br/>" + yahooObject.ResultSet.Result[1].Summary
                      + "<hr size=1 noshade color=#CFCFCF>";
                    html = html + "<a href="
                      + yahooObject.ResultSet.Result[2].Url
                      + " target=_yaoo>"
                      + yahooObject.ResultSet.Result[2].Title + "</a><br/>"
                      + yahooObject.ResultSet.Result[2].Summary;

                    document.getElementById("myYahooResult").innerHTML = html;
                }
            });
    }
```

If you're faced with a JSON string without any API documentation, look for opening and closing brackets. This will immediately give you the intended object definition. Then look for the name/value pairs enclosed in the brackets.

Remember, brackets and name/value pairs must be balanced in a properly defined JSON response.

Servlet layer

Finally, we have the code for the Servlet layer.

We could ask why we introduce a Servlet layer between the HTML and the actual web services. In other words, why don't we just make Ajax calls from the view to directly connect to each API? For security reasons, JavaScript, by design, doesn't allow Ajax calls to execute from different domains where the original HTTP request comes from (though there are ways to bypass this security constraint using Prototype). Therefore, in our application, the Servlets are the local proxy to the remote web services.

SemanticHacker parser Servlet

As noted in our application directory structure, we have five Servlets. The code listings are presented in this section, and we begin with the full code listing for `MySemanticSearch.java`:

```java
import java.io.IOException;
import java.io.PrintWriter;

import javax.servlet.ServletException;
import javax.servlet.http.HttpServlet;
import javax.servlet.http.HttpServletRequest;
import javax.servlet.http.HttpServletResponse;

import java.net.URLEncoder;

import org.apache.commons.httpclient.HttpClient;
import org.apache.commons.httpclient.HttpStatus;
import org.apache.commons.httpclient.methods.PostMethod;
import org.apache.commons.httpclient.methods.StringRequestEntity;

public class MySemanticParse extends HttpServlet {
    // Note that you will need your own key to run
    //    this application locally.
    // You can get a free key from http://api.semantichacker.com/
    private static final String URI = «http://api.semantichacker.com
        /YOUR_API_KEY/concept?format=tagcloud»;
    private static final String CONTENT_TYPE = «text/html»;
    private static final String CHAR_ENCODING = «UTF-8»;

    public void doPost(HttpServletRequest request,
        HttpServletResponse response) throws ServletException,
            IOException {
        response.setContentType(CONTENT_TYPE);
        PrintWriter out = response.getWriter();
        PostMethod postMethod = null;
        try {
            String entry = URLEncoder.encode(request
                .getParameter(«entry»), CHAR_ENCODING);
            postMethod = new PostMethod(URI);
            postMethod.setRequestEntity(new StringRequestEntity(
                entry, CONTENT_TYPE, CHAR_ENCODING));

            HttpClient httpClient = new HttpClient();
            int statusCode = httpClient.executeMethod(postMethod);

            if (statusCode == HttpStatus.SC_OK) {
                String semanticResponse = new
                    String(postMethod.getResponseBody());
```

```
                    // Set top cloud value
                    String tmp1 = semanticResponse.substring
                        (semanticResponse.indexOf(«title=\»») + 7);
                    String topCloud = tmp1.substring(0, tmp1
                        .indexOf('(')).trim();
                    request.getSession(true).setAttribute(«TOP_CLOUD»,
                        topCloud);

                    // Sent to out stream
                    out.print(semanticResponse);
                } else {
                    out.print(«HTTP error with code: « + statusCode);
                }
            } catch (Exception e) {
                // Send any errors to the view
                out.print(e.getMessage());
            } finally {
                if (postMethod != null) {
                    postMethod.releaseConnection();
                }
            }
        }
    }
}
```

We first parse the entry's value with our SemanticHacker API and we set an attribute in the `HttpSession` object for further processing by two other Servlets.

A call to the service with a value to parse of "java" returns the following HTML:

```
<ul class="tw-cloud">
    <li class="size6">
        <a rel="tag" href="http://delicious.com/tag/java"
            target="_blank" title="java (1.000)">
            <span>java <em>(1.000)</em></span>
        </a>
    </li>
</ul>
```

Because we need the most relevant topic to further search the Web with other services, we need to get it out from this result. To harvest this top cloud, we code a quick and dirty string parser to look for it (proper error checking is omitted for the sake of brevity). We then store the value in the `HttpSession` object as an attribute with the key TOP_CLOUD with the following code:

```
String semanticResponse = new
    String(postMethod.getResponseBody());

// Set top cloud value
```

```
String tmp1 = semanticResponse.substring(semanticResponse
    .indexOf("title=\"") + 7);
String topCloud = tmp1.substring(0, tmp1.indexOf('(')).trim();
request.getSession(true).setAttribute("TOP_CLOUD", topCloud);
```

Relevancy is indicated by the value enclosed in parenthesis. For this example, we have a tag cloud with the value of "java" and relevancy of 1.00 (for full details, see http://www.semantichacker.com/api).

 Even though we store the value of the top cloud in the session object, this is not recommended. We use this coding style for the sake of clarity and brevity.

Google search Servlet

The full code listing for MyGoogleSearch.java looks like:

```
import java.io.IOException;
import java.io.PrintWriter;

import javax.servlet.ServletException;
import javax.servlet.http.HttpServlet;
import javax.servlet.http.HttpServletRequest;
import javax.servlet.http.HttpServletResponse;

import java.net.URLEncoder ;

import org.apache.commons.httpclient.HttpClient;
import org.apache.commons.httpclient.HttpStatus;
import org.apache.commons.httpclient.methods.GetMethod;

public class MyGoogleSearch extends HttpServlet {
    private static final String URI = «http://ajax.googleapis.com
        /ajax/services/search/web?v=1.0&q=»;
    private static final String CONTENT_TYPE = «text/javascript»;
    private static final String CHAR_ENCODING = «UTF-8»;

    public void doGet(HttpServletRequest request, HttpServletResponse
        response) throws ServletException, IOException {
        response.setContentType(CONTENT_TYPE);
        PrintWriter out = response.getWriter();
        GetMethod getMethod = null;
        try {
            String topCloud = request.getSession()
                .getAttribute(«TOP_CLOUD»).toString();

            // Only search if we have top cloud
```

```
            if ((topCloud != null) && !topCloud.isEmpty()) {
                String q = URLEncoder.encode(topCloud,
                    CHAR_ENCODING);
                getMethod = new GetMethod(URI + q);
                HttpClient httpClient = new HttpClient();
                int statusCode = httpClient.executeMethod(getMethod);
                if (statusCode == HttpStatus.SC_OK) {
                    out.print(new String(getMethod
                        .getResponseBody()));
                } else {
                    out.print(«HTTP error with code: « + statusCode);
                }
            }
        } catch (Exception e) {
            // Send any errors to the view
            out.print(e.getMessage());
        } finally {
            if (getMethod != null) {
                getMethod.releaseConnection();
            }
        }
    }
}
```

As we mentioned, we store the top cloud in the HttpSession object with the key
TOP_CLOUD. We now retrieve it from the session and execute a Google search—by
default Google's service returns a JSON representation.

We've been saying that we don't parse the result at the Servlet layer. We can see
what that means here: we just pass the result of the API to the caller of the Servlet by
setting the content type to text/javascript and sending the result on the response
out stream.

Twitter search Servlet

The full code listing for MyTwitterSearch.java looks as follows:

```
import java.io.IOException;
import java.io.PrintWriter;

import javax.servlet.ServletException;
import javax.servlet.http.HttpServlet;
import javax.servlet.http.HttpServletRequest;
import javax.servlet.http.HttpServletResponse;

import java.net.URLEncoder;

import org.apache.commons.httpclient.HttpClient;
```

```
import org.apache.commons.httpclient.HttpStatus;
import org.apache.commons.httpclient.methods.GetMethod;
public class MyTwitterSearch extends HttpServlet {
    private static final String URI =
        «http://search.twitter.com/search.json?q=»;
    private static final String CONTENT_TYPE = «text/javascript»;
    private static final String CHAR_ENCODING = «UTF-8»;
    public void doGet(HttpServletRequest request, HttpServletResponse
        response) throws ServletException, IOException {
        response.setContentType(CONTENT_TYPE);
        PrintWriter out = response.getWriter();
        GetMethod getMethod = null;
        try {
            String topCloud = request.getSession()
                .getAttribute(«TOP_CLOUD»).toString();

            // Only search if we have top cloud
            if ((topCloud != null) && !topCloud.isEmpty()) {
                String q = URLEncoder.encode(topCloud,
                    CHAR_ENCODING);
                getMethod = new GetMethod(URI + q);

                HttpClient httpClient = new HttpClient();
                int statusCode = httpClient.executeMethod(getMethod);

                if (statusCode == HttpStatus.SC_OK) {
                    out.print(new String(getMethod
                        .getResponseBody()));
                } else {
                    out.print(«HTTP error with code: « + statusCode);
                }
            }
        } catch (Exception e) {
            // Send any errors to the view
            out.print(e.getMessage());
        } finally {
            if (getMethod != null) {
                getMethod.releaseConnection();
            }
        }
    }
}
```

Similar to our Google search Servlet, this class connects to Twitter's web service to search for the value of the top cloud stored in the `HttpSession` object, and then passes the result to the caller.

Yahoo search Servlet

The full code listing for `MyYahooSearch.java` looks as follows:

```java
import java.io.IOException;
import java.io.PrintWriter;

import javax.servlet.ServletException;
import javax.servlet.http.HttpServlet;
import javax.servlet.http.HttpServletRequest;
import javax.servlet.http.HttpServletResponse;

import java.net.URLEncoder;

import org.apache.commons.httpclient.HttpClient;
import org.apache.commons.httpclient.HttpStatus;
import org.apache.commons.httpclient.methods.GetMethod;

public class MyYahooSearch extends HttpServlet {
    // Note that 'appid=YahooDemo' should be your own appid
    private static final String URI = «http://search.yahooapis.com
        /WebSearchService/V1/webSearch
            ?output=json&appid=YahooDemo&query=»;
    private static final String CONTENT_TYPE = «text/javascript»;
    private static final String CHAR_ENCODING = «UTF-8»;
    public void doGet(HttpServletRequest request, HttpServletResponse
        response) throws ServletException, IOException {
        response.setContentType(CONTENT_TYPE);
        PrintWriter out = response.getWriter();
        GetMethod getMethod = null;
        try {
            String query = URLEncoder.encode(request
                .getParameter(«query»), CHAR_ENCODING);
            getMethod = new GetMethod(URI + query);
            HttpClient httpClient = new HttpClient();
            int statusCode = httpClient.executeMethod(getMethod);
            if (statusCode == HttpStatus.SC_OK) {
                out.print(new String(getMethod.getResponseBody()));
            } else {
                out.print(«HTTP error with code: « + statusCode);
            }
        } catch (Exception e) {
            // Send any errors to the view
            out.print(e.getMessage());
        } finally {
            if (getMethod != null) {
                getMethod.releaseConnection();
            }
        }
    }
}
```

The difference between this Servlet and the previous ones is that we look for the value of the search query in the `HttpServletRequest` object. In other words, the search term is a parameter in the GET request with a name/value pair of key `query`.

Yahoo image search Servlet

The full code listing for `MyYahooImageSearch.java` looks as follows:

```java
import java.io.IOException;
import java.io.PrintWriter;

import javax.servlet.ServletException;
import javax.servlet.http.HttpServlet;
import javax.servlet.http.HttpServletRequest;
import javax.servlet.http.HttpServletResponse;

import java.net.URLEncoder;

import org.apache.commons.httpclient.HttpClient;
import org.apache.commons.httpclient.HttpStatus;
import org.apache.commons.httpclient.methods.GetMethod;

public class MyYahooImageSearch extends HttpServlet {
    // Note that 'appid=YahooDemo' should be your own appid if you
    //    want to create a real application
    private static final String URI = "http://search.yahooapis.com
        /ImageSearchService/V1/imageSearch
            ?output=json&appid=YahooDemo&query=";
    private static final String CONTENT_TYPE = "text/javascript";
    private static final String CHAR_ENCODING = "UTF-8";
    public void doGet(HttpServletRequest request, HttpServletResponse
        response) throws ServletException, IOException {
        response.setContentType(CONTENT_TYPE);
        PrintWriter out = response.getWriter();
        GetMethod getMethod = null;
        try {
            String query = URLEncoder.encode(request
                .getParameter("query"), CHAR_ENCODING);
            getMethod = new GetMethod(URI + query);
            HttpClient httpClient = new HttpClient();
            int statusCode = httpClient.executeMethod(getMethod);
            if (statusCode == HttpStatus.SC_OK) {
                out.print(new String(getMethod.getResponseBody()));
            } else {
                out.print("HTTP error with code: " + statusCode);
            }
        } catch (Exception e) {
            // Send any errors to the view
```

```
            out.print(e.getMessage());
        } finally {
            if (getMethod != null) {
                getMethod.releaseConnection();
            }
        }
    }
}
```

The only difference between this Servlet and `MyYahooSearch` is the search URI.

Compiling and running the application

We have five Servlets to compile. Assuming we have the directory tree specified earlier and we are inside the `classes` directory with all our libraries and source files in it, we compile the application with the following command:

```
javac -classpath "/apache-tomcat-6.0.16/lib/servlet-api.jar;commons-
logging-1.1.1.jar;commons-codec-1.3.jar;commons-httpclient-3.1.jar"
*.java
```

To run the application, we copy the `RESTfulMashupSearch` directory to the `webapps` directory (in Tomcat, for example), restart the web server, and then point our browser to `http://localhost:8080/RESTfulMashupSearch/`, assuming the server is running in the 8080 port. (Again, a deployable application is part of the downloadable package.)

Summary

Our semantic web application uses multiple RESTful and REST like web services. As we have seen, some of these services don't adhere to all the constraints that make a RESTful architecture. Nevertheless, we can still use them in RESTful clients because they use HTTP as the mode of transport at the application layer.

With more than enough client development covered in Chapter 2 and Chapter 3, we now switch gears and move to the world of design and implementation of fully compliant RESTful web services.

4
RESTful Web Services Design

The RESTful development process follows traditional development paradigms. However, with RESTful web services, we need to analyze the resource requirements first, design the representation for our resources second, identify the URIs third, and, lastly, worry about implementation technologies.

Throughout this book we've talked about creating web services that are noun dependent as opposed to verb dependent. In this chapter we'll look at what that means in terms of the design process. For this, we'll design a blogging application, but we'll leave the implementation for later chapters. Our sample application is a micro-blogging web service (similar to Twitter), where users create accounts and then post entries.

Finally, while designing our application, we'll define a set of steps that can be applied to designing any software system that needs to be deployed as a RESTful web service.

Designing a RESTful web service

Designing RESTful web services is not different from designing traditional web applications. We still have business requirements, we still have users who want to do things with data, and we still have hardware constraints and software architectures to deal with. The main difference, however, is that we look at the requirements to tease out resources and forget about specific actions to be taken on these resources.

We can think of RESTful web service design as being similar to Object Oriented Design (OOD). In OOD, we try to identify objects from the data we want to represent together with the actions that an object can have. But the similarities end at the data structure definition, because with RESTful web services we already have specific calls that are part of the protocol itself.

The underlying RESTful web service design principles can be summarized in the following four steps:

1. **Requirements gathering**—this step is similar to traditional software requirement gathering practices.

2. **Resource identification**—this step is similar to OOD where we identify objects, but we don't worry about messaging between objects.

3. **Resource representation definition**—because we exchange representation between clients and servers, we should define what kind of representation we need to use. Typically, we use XML, but JSON has gained popularity. That's not to say that we can't use any other form of resource representation—on the contrary, we could use XHTML or any other form of binary representation, though we let the requirements guide our choices.

4. **URI definition**—with resources in place, we need to define the API, which consists of URIs for clients and servers to exchange resources' representations.

This design process is not static. These are iterative steps that gravitate around resources. Let's say that during the *URI definition* step we discover that one of the URI's responses is not covered in one of the resources we have identified. Then we go back to define a suitable resource. In most cases, however, we find that the resources that we already have cover most of our needs, and we just have to combine existing resources into a meta-resource to take care of the new requirement.

Requirements of sample web service

The RESTful web service we design in this chapter is a social networking web application similar to Twitter.

Throughout this book, we follow an OOD process mixed with an agile philosophy for designing and coding our applications. This means that we create just enough documentation to be useful, but not so much that we spend an inordinate amount of time deciphering it during our implementation phase.

As with any application, we begin by listing the main business requirements, for which we have the following use cases (these are the main functions of our application):

- A web user creates an account with a username and a password (creating an account means that the user is now registered).
- Registered users post blog entries to their accounts. We limit messages to 140 characters.
- Registered and non-registered users view all blog entries.
- Registered and non-registered users view user profiles.
- Registered users update their user profiles, for example, users update their password.
- Registered and non-registered users search for terms in all blog entries.

However simple this example may be, social networking sites work on these same principles: users sign up for accounts to post personal updates or information. Our intention here, though, is not to fully replicate Twitter or to fully create a social networking application. What we are trying to outline is a set of requirements that will test our understanding of RESTful web services design and implementation.

The core value of social networking sites lies in the ability to connect to multiple users who connect with us, and the value is derived from what the connections mean within the community, because of the tendency of users following people with similar interests. For example, the connections between users create targeted distribution networks.

The connections between users create random graphs in the *graph theory* sense, where nodes are users and edges are connections between users. This is what is referred to as the *social graph*.

Resource identification

Out of the use cases listed above, we now need to define the service's resources. From reading the requirements we see that we need users and messages. Users appear in two ways: a single user and a list of users. Additionally, users have the ability to post blog entries in the form of messages of no more than 140 characters. This means that we need resources for a single message and a list of messages. In sum, we identify the following resources:

- User
- List of users
- Message
- List of messages

Representation definition

As we discussed in our introduction to RESTful web services, a representation is a temporal mapping of a resource at the time of a request. Furthermore, a representation is transmitted between clients and servers over HTTP. Because of HTTP's flexibility, any binary stream can be transferred. Nevertheless, we don't recommend choosing just any type of binary representation that requires special code or libraries to consume. We recommend using primarily XML and JSON structures, remembering, of course, that the requirements of the problem we're solving dictate what representation types we must provide.

A well-designed RESTful web service needs to provide multiple resource representations. We can't assume that only web browsers will be accessing our public APIs or that only the one type of client we identified in our *requirement gathering* process will use our services.

What are the options available, then?

Again, arriving at the ideal representation format is a matter of the design process. We need to take into account what the service is doing and what clients will be using the resources for. The safest representation format is therefore XML. This is what web services are known for: transferring XML streams over web transport protocols. More important, most programming languages already have libraries available to parse XML streams.

Finally, we need to account for linkability of representations. Linkability of representation means that the web services provide for resource discoverability, such that resources link to other resources (what's currently being referred to as **HATEOS** or **Hypermedia As The Engine Of State transfer**). For example, our URI for a list of users returns a structure of users with each element in the list having a direct URI to each element in the service (a link to a user).

XML representations

From our analysis, we identified two types of resources: users and messages. As part of the heuristics we outlined earlier, we need to define what our representation will look like. The following representations are the structures that we will have to implement when we actually code the web service.

Users

We first define a user representation as follows:

```
<user>
  <username></username>
  <password></password>
  <link></link>
</user>
```

As part of a user resource, we store only a username and a password. The username is unique in the context of our system and is used to uniquely identify each user. The link element, which points back to the web service, is either assigned when the resource is created or a representation is built for transport (for our sample service, we let the backend create the link).

We now define a list of users as follows:

```
<users>
<count></count>
<link></link>
    <user>
        <username></username>
        <password></password>
        <link></link>
    </user>
    ...
    <user>
        <username></username>
        <password></password>
        <link></link>
    </user>
</users>
```

This XML structure declares a list of users stored in an XML element <users>. We use ellipses or . . . to show that we can have more than one user in the list.

 We can see here the linkability concept at play: with a list of users we can drill down to individual users using the link element's value.

Messages

We first define a single blog entry or message as follows:

```
<message>
    <messageID></messageID>
    <content></content>
    <link></link>
    <user>
        <username></username>
        <password></password>
        <link></link>
    </user>
</message>
```

A message needs a message id, the body of the message (the content element), and the user who posted the message. Note that depending on what we are doing with the message, we don't pass all the resource's information back and forth. For example, when we are creating a message at the client layer, we don't know what the value for messageID is. Therefore, we still need to pass the message structure to the service, but our web service will know that any messageID value needs to be ignored, because, in our case, it will be created by the storage layer.

Finally, we define a list of messages as follows:

```
<messages>
    <count></count>
    <link></link>
    <message>
        <messageID></messageID>
        <content></content>
        <link></link>
        <user>
            <username></username>
            <password></password>
            <link></link>
        </user>
    </message>
    ...
    <message>
        <messageID></messageID>
        <content></content>
        <link></link>
        <user>
            <username></username>
            <password></password>
            <link></link>
        </user>
    </message>
</messages>
```

This XML structure holds a collection of messages, and each message holds the user who posted the message.

 We use the XML representation type for input and output. Input in this case means that we send a resource representation to create and update the resources at the web service layer in the form of an XML object. Output means that a client requests an XML representation of a resource.

JSON representations

We use the same key names for our JSON representation, and we still have only two types of resources: users and messages. Again, these structures are our specification of what we need to return for each request.

Users

We define a user representation as follows:

```
{"user":{"username":"john", "password":"password", "link":"/users/
john"}}
```

And we define a list of users as follows (we use the . . . characters to show that there is more than one user in the array):

```
{"users-result":{"count":"6", "users":[{"username":"john",
"password":"password", "link":"/users/john"}, ...,{"username":"jane",
"password":"password", "link":"/users/jane"}]}}
```

The array for all users as a JSON structure, looks as follows:

```
"users":[{"username":"john", "password":"password", "link":"/users/
john"}, ...,{"username":"jane", "password":"password", "link":"/users/
jane"}]
```

Once the JSON response has been evaluated with the JavaScript `eval()` function, similar to what we did in Chapters 2 and 3, we can then access any of the values in the structure. For example, if we need the user name of the first element on the array, we use `users-result.users[0].username`.

Messages

We now define a message representation as follows:

```
{"message":{"messageID":"some-id", "content":"some content",
"link":"/messages/some-id", "user":{"user":{"username":"john",
"password":"password", "link":"/users/john"}}}
```

And a list of messages as follows:

```
{"messages-result":{"count":"6", "link":"/messages",
"messages":[{"messageID":"some-id", "content":"some content",
"link":"/messages/some-id", "user":{"username":"john",
"password":"password", "link":"/users/john"}}, ...,{"messageID":"some-
id2", "content":"some content", "link":"/messages/some-id2",
"user":{"username":"jane", "password":"password", "link":"/users/
jane"}}]}}
```

Each message element in the array has a user structure embedded as follows:

```
{"messageID":"some-id", "content":"some content",
"user":{"username":"john", "password":"password", "link":"/users/
john"}}
```

Once the JSON response has been evaluated with the JavaScript `eval()` function, we can then access the first element on the list with `messages-result.messages[0].content`; if we want to get the user name of the user who posted the message, we access the value with `messages-result.messages[0].user.username`.

> Note that during implementation we'll use JSON representations only as response streams. This means that we won't use JSON structures to create or update resources at the web service layer. Although we could use XML and JSON to update resources at the service layer, we'll omit JSON for the sake of brevity.

URI definition

The next step involves the definition of URIs. This is a crucial step, as the URIs define our API and it's likely that we want to make our web service public.

We strive to make our APIs logical, hierarchical, and as permanent as we can. We must emphasize these three tenets, as we may have many developers depending on the services we make available. Therefore, a good API is one that doesn't change too often and is unambiguous to use. Furthermore, the idea of RESTful APIs is that we maintain URI uniqueness and reliability of service. (For a complete discussion about this topic, see `http://www.w3.org/Provider/Style/URI`.)

The first thing we need is a web address. In our case, we assume that we're using our development machine running on `http://localhost:8080/`.

It's important to distinguish between a web service and a web application: we use web services to implement web applications, and web services can be, and are recommended to be, independent of web applications. What's more, web applications are meant to be consumed by humans, as opposed to web services that are intended for machine consumption.

For example, a RESTful API could live under `http://api.restfuljava.com/` and a web application using the API could live under `http://restfuljava.com/`. Both the API and the web application should be running on independent hardware for performance reasons, but when we get to implement our sample service we run everything on the same server.

The nomenclature of RESTful URIs falls under the topic of URI templates and the following conventions are widely used. First, for items or identifiers that don't change, we find the keyword to be part of the actual URI—for instance, we use `users` to be the URI for a list of all users. Second, we use keys or dynamic keywords to be enclosed in { and }. Applying these conventions, our URI list for users looks as follows:

- `http://localhost:8080/users`—with the GET method, this URI returns a list of all users; with the POST method, we create a new user and the payload is a user's XML representation; we don't support the PUT method; finally, we don't support the DELETE method for an entire list of users

- `http://localhost:8080/users/{username}`—with the GET method, this URI returns a representation of a user with a unique identifier `username`; with the PUT method, it updates a user; and, with the DELETE method, it deletes a user.

And for messages, our URI list looks as follows:

- `http://localhost:8080/messages`—with the GET method, this URI returns a list of all messages from all users; with the POST method, it creates a new message, with the message's XML representation as the payload of the request

- `http://localhost:8080/messages/{messageID}`—with the GET method, this URI returns a representation for a message with the unique identifier `messageID`; with the DELETE method, it deletes a message; and we don't support the POST or PUT methods

- `http://localhost:8080/messages/users/{username}`—with the GET method, this URI returns a list of all message for a user with identifier `username`; no POST, PUT, or DELETE methods are supported

At the time of this writing, the URI Template specification is still under review. For more information, see `http://tools.ietf.org/html/draft-gregorio-uritemplate-03`.

Executing logic with RESTful URIs

A question arises when designing RESTful web services that has to do with executing code at the server level. Specifically, how do we execute logic if we limit our client/server interactions to only four CRUD-like calls (POST, GET, PUT, and DELETE)? For this we need to introduce URIs that execute logic on the server, remembering that responses must be in the form of resource representations. In other words, we avoid any RPC style calls and concentrate on the resources only.

For our web service, we only offer the ability of searching for a term or a phrase in the blog entries. For example, any user can search for the term "programming" or "software development" using the following URI (note that the URI pattern is arbitrary and you can choose whatever makes sense for the service you are developing):

```
http://localhost:8080/messages/search/{search_item}
```

This URI returns a list of messages that contain the word or words search_item—this is strictly a GET method call and no POST, PUT, or DELETE method is supported

Using URIs to request representation types

A RESTful web service is one that adheres to all the constraints we outlined in Chapter 1, *RESTful Architectures*. However, we have encountered APIs that don't strictly adhere to every constraint. For example, requesting representation types via URIs is something we saw with Twitter's API. We requested three different types of representations with the URI http://twitter.com/statuses/public_timeline. {xml, json, rss}.

We said that this is not technically a RESTful web service request, because we don't use the communication protocol—HTTP headers—to tell the service what kind of representation to get. Even though this is not a RESTful web service, it still works. Nevertheless, the API may be open to interpretation. For example, what does it mean to send an HTTP GET request to the URI http://twitter.com/statuses/ public_timeline.json with an HTTP *Accept* header value of application/xml? Do we get a JSON representation or an XML representation? A properly designed RESTful web service has to adhere to *all* REST constraints, and using the protocol to negotiate representations is part of being RESTful.

Creating a properly defined RESTful web service, however, ensures that there are no misunderstandings on how to use such services. For example, setting the HTTP method type to GET with an appropriate *Accept* header value makes it clear that we are requesting a resource of a specific type. In the end, you, as a developer or software architect, need to make a decision as to which style will benefit your users the most.

Using this representation request style is a design decision that facilitates—it can be argued—the writing of clients. For instance, the majority of public APIs are read only, so using a straight HTTP GET request with the type of representation embedded in the URI is easier than instantiating a full HTTP request and modifying the HTTP header *Accept* each time. Note that neither is hard to implement; however, with the former, we save a couple of lines of code at the client layer. Again, it's a matter of choice.

 Our sample web service is a canonical application, thus we don't deviate from any of the constraints. This means that we use the HTTP protocol to request a preferred resource representation and not the URI style described in this section.

Summary

As we've seen, the RESTful design process is resource centric. In addition, we have no arbitrary actions executing on the data—we have HTTP method calls that exchange representations using clearly defined URIs.

The steps to arrive at a web service that adheres to all REST constraints are similar to traditional web application design. So we can still use all our traditional requirement gathering techniques, but tweak the process to account for proper design of usable URIs and consumable representations.

Now that we have our social networking web service specification defined together with a set of RESTful design principles, the next step is implementation. We have four different REST frameworks in the menu, so in the next chapter we begin with Jersey, which is the reference implementation of the Java API for RESTful Web Services Specification, more commonly known as JAX-RS.

5
Jersey: JAX-RS

In the world of RESTful web services, we have a few pure Java RESTful frameworks available. Among them we have Jersey, the reference implementation of Sun's Java API for RESTful Web Services—more commonly known as JAX-RS.

In this chapter, we use Jersey to implement the web service we defined in Chapter 4, *RESTful Web Services Design*. We leave no detail out: we begin with an introduction to Jersey and how it provides the plumbing to create RESTful web services, and end with the dissection of all the code necessary to program our web application.

Finally, because this is one of four Java RESTful frameworks we are studying in this book, we break down the implementation into layers that are interchangeable. For example, we'll be able to reuse a large portion of the code we develop in this chapter and conveniently plug in different RESTful web layers in subsequent chapters.

Getting the tools

For this chapter, we need to download two software packages, assuming the latest Java JDK and Tomcat web container are already installed. We need D4bo, an open source non-relational database; and Jersey, the reference implementation of the JAX-RS API. The complete list of tools together with their download locations is as follows:

Software	Web location
Java JDK	`http://java.sun.com/`
Apache Tomcat	`http://tomcat.apache.org/download-60.cgi`
Db4o	`http://developer.db4o.com/files/default.aspx`
Jersey Framework	`https://jersey.dev.java.net/`

Install the latest Java JDK together with the latest version of Tomcat, if you haven't done so. Download and install Db4o and Jersey. Remember the location of the installs, as we'll need some of the libraries to be deployed with our web application.

JAX-RS

The Java technology stack has always been part of web service solutions, but it was limited to WSDL and SOAP. With the advent of REST, the JAX-RS project was started by the **Java Community Process (JCP)** with the goal of creating an API for Java RESTful web services. The API is also known as JAX-311 or JAX-RS. This specification is used by anyone wishing to create a Java framework that adheres to all the REST constraints we've looked at.

Jersey the JAX-RS 1.1 reference implementation

A reference implementation is one that implements all the requirements in a particular specification. Reference implementations don't start with production performance in mind, because they must implement every detail outlined. Nevertheless, Jersey has evolved into a viable option for deploying RESTful web services.

There are two released versions of Jersey at the time of this writing, though we're only covering version 1.1. One of the goals of the JAX-RS group is to provide a container agnostic specification and therefore Jersey works with any JEE server. Consequently, for the purpose of this book, we'll stick with Tomcat, as we're already familiar with it.

 Jersey is an open source project and is constantly being updated. If you would like to contribute, visit `https://jersey.dev.java.net/`.

Annotations

The main goal of the JAX-RS specification is to make RESTful web service development easier than it has been in the past. Jersey provides the connectors for web services through Java annotations—annotations automatically generate the code necessary for classes that use them to seamlessly connect within specific frameworks (for details on annotation, see `http://java.sun.com/j2se/1.5.0/docs/guide/language/annotations.html`).

The use of annotations allows us to create Jersey resources just as easily as we develop Plain Old Java Objects (POJOs). In other words, we leave the intercepting of HTTP requests and representation negotiations to the framework and we can then concentrate on the business rules necessary to solve our problem at hand.

Before coding our web service, let's look at the annotations Jersey provides, as defined in the JAX-311 specification. The snippets of code shown for every annotation in this section are only samples and are not meant to be implemented or to run standalone. The full implementation of the web service is in the next section, so if you are already familiar with Jersey's annotations, it's safe to skip the rest of this section.

Jersey resource

A Jersey resource is a plain Java class within the context of a web application that uses the `@Path` annotation to define a URI. The value of the annotation is the URI relative to the web application context, as deployed in the web server.

URIs

Every Jersey resource has a URI pointing to it. A resource is identified with the `@Path` annotation.

@Path

One of the URIs we define in our web service specification is `/users` (this URI points to the representation of a list of users). In code, using this annotation looks as follows:

```
@Path("/users")
public class UsersResource {
}
```

This annotation is also used to define variables in URIs. If we recall, we said that a URI for a specific user looks like `/users/{username}`, so in code this looks as follows:

```
@Path("/users/{username}")
public class UserResource {
}
```

These are two different resources: the former is to access a list of users, and the latter is to access a single user that has the identifier `username`.

With the use of regular expressions, the `@Path` annotation can also be used to limit the values URIs can have. For example, we could limit the value of `username` to contain only alpha characters as follows:

```
@Path("/users/{username: [a-zA-Z]}")
public class UserResource {
}
```

HTTP methods

Every HTTP request made to a web service is handled by an appropriately annotated method in a resource class, provided that the resource class has the annotation `@Path` defined. Jersey supports the following annotations for each one of the HTTP method requests.

@GET

An HTTP GET request is handled by an annotated method that looks as follows:

```
@Path("/users")
public class UserResource {
    @GET
    public String handleGETRequest() {
    }
}
```

The name of the method is not important. However, we should use descriptive names that are representative of the problem we are solving.

@POST

An HTTP POST request is handled by an annotated method that looks as follows:

```
@Path("/users")
public class UserResource {
    @POST
    public String handlePOSTRequest(String payload) {
    }
}
```

The POST request has a payload that the framework intercepts and delivers to us in the parameter `payload`. The value of the payload could be an XML structure, so we use a String object. However, the payload could also be a binary stream of, say, MIME type `image/jpg`, so our object type for the payload must change accordingly (`InputStream`, for instance). Note that the name of the payload variable is arbitrary, just like the name of the method containing it.

@PUT

An HTTP PUT request is handled by an annotated method that looks as follows:

```
@Path("/users")
public class UserResource {
    @PUT
    public String handlePUTRequest(String payload) {
    }
}
```

Similar to the POST request, the PUT request has a payload associated with it, which is stored in the `payload` variable.

@DELETE

An HTTP DELETE request is handled by an annotated method that looks as follows:

```
@Path("/users")
public class UserResource {
    @DELETE
    public void handleDELETERequest() {
    }
}
```

For now, ignore the return type of each of these methods. We'll cover that with the `@Produces` annotation in the next section.

Relative paths in methods

We can also have relative paths for each method from the root path annotated in the definition of the class. For example, this resource class serves URIs to /users:

```
@Path("/users")
public class UserResource {
    @GET
    public String handleGETRequest() {
    }
}
```

If we wanted to serve the URI /users/messages, for example, we don't need a new class definition, and we could annotate a new method handleGETRequestMessages() as follows:

```
@Path("/users")
public class UserResource {
    @GET
    public String handleGETRequest() {
    }

    @GET @Path("/messages")
    public String handleGETRequestMessages() {
    }
}
```

We now have one resource class that handles requests for /users and /users/messages/.

URI variables

@PathParam

This annotation is used together with @Path and in conjunction with @GET, @POST, @PUT, and @DELETE.

In our specification, we have the URI /users/{username}. We said that username is a variable, but how do we get the value from the URI?

This is where the @PathParam comes into play. Using this annotation with the HTTP methods GET, POST, PUT, and DELETE looks as follows:

```
@Path("/users/{username}")
public class UserResource {
    @GET
```

```
    public String handleGET(@PathParam("username") String username) {
        // We can use username however we like...
    }

    @POST
    public String handlePOST(@PathParam("username") String username) {
    }

    @PUT
    public String handlePUT(@PathParam("username") String username) {
}

    @DELETE
    public String handleDELETE(@PathParam("username") String
        username) {
    }
}
```

`@PathParam` gives us access to the value of the variable, but we have to define a String object as part of the method signature. Once defined, `username` is just another variable within the scope of the method. Note that the String variable doesn't have to have the same name as the variable in the URI. Nevertheless, we use the same names of the URI variables and object instances throughout this chapter to be consistent (consistent names make debugging easier).

We can also use multiple variables in our URIs. For example, we could have a URI to query for a list of users that limits the results by gender, age, and address that looks like `/users/{gender}/{age}/{address}`. Then our method definition would look as follows:

```
@Path("/users/{gender}/{age}/{address}")
public class UsersResource {
    @GET
    public String handleGET(@PathParam("gender") String gender,
        @PathParam("age") int age, @PathParam("address")
            String address) {
    }
}
```

Depending on the requirements of our web service, we don't use the `@PathParam` annotation with a POST request. In some cases, we don't let the client dictate the unique identifier of the resource during creation time; we're more likely to let the backend decide the value of the identifier for each resource, just like we do for messages.

Input and output formats

We know how to handle requests made to a web service; we now need to figure out how to exchange inbound and outbound representations between clients and servers. For this, we have the following annotations.

@Consumes

This annotation works together with @POST and @PUT. It tells the framework to which method to delegate the incoming request. Specifically, the client sets the *Content-Type* HTTP header and the framework delegates the request to the corresponding handling method. An example of this annotation together with @PUT looks as follows:

```
@Path("/users")
public class UserResource {
    @PUT
    @Consumes("application/xml")
    public void updateUser(String representation) {
    }
}
```

In this example we're telling the framework that the updateUser() method accepts an input stream of MIME type application/xml, which is stored in the variable representation. Therefore, a client connecting to the web service through the URI /users must send an HTTP PUT method request containing the HTTP header *Content-Type* with a value of application/xml.

A resource can accept different types of payloads. Thus, we use the @PUT annotation with multiple methods to handle requests with different MIME types. So, we could have the following, a method to accept XML structures and a method to accept JSON structures:

```
@Path("/users")
public class UserResource {
    @PUT
    @Consumes("application/xml")
    public void updateXML(String representation) {
    }
    @PUT
    @Consumes("application/json")
    public void updateJSON(String representation) {
    }
}
```

Again, the client must provide the MIME type it's sending to the web service. The job of the framework is to delegate the incoming HTTP request to the method matching the intended MIME type.

For @POST we use the same idea:

```
@Path("/users")
public class UserResource {
    @POST
    @Consumes("application/xml")
    public void updateXML(String representation) {
    }

    @POST
    @Consumes("application/json")
    public void updateJSON(String representation) {
    }
}
```

@Produces

This annotation works with @GET, @POST, and @PUT. It lets the framework know what type of representation to send back to the client.

Specifically, the client sends an HTTP request together with an Accept HTTP header that maps directly to the *Content-Type* the method produces. So, if the value of the HTTP header *Accept* is application/xml, the method handling the request returns a stream of MIME type application/xml. This annotation can also be used with multiple methods in the same resource class. An example that returns XML and JSON representations looks as follows:

```
@Path("/users")
public class UserResource {
    @GET
    @Produces("application/xml")
    public String getXML(String representation) {
    }

    @GET
    @Produces("application/json")
    public String getJSON(String representation) {
    }
}
```

 If a client sends a request to a URI with a MIME type that is not supported by the resource, then an appropriate exception is thrown by Jersey.

Parameters

RESTful web services exchange representations using URIs. However, because
we use web technologies and because of design decisions, we don't always use
representation such as XML structures. We sometimes need to provide other
means to transfer data such as plain HTML forms. This means that if a client sends
a request from an HTML form, we need to get access to the value/pair set that is
part of the request. Even though we don't use the following annotation in our web
service, you may want to take a look at it and then decide if it makes sense to use in
your solutions.

@FormParam

This annotation lets us read the values of name/value pairs passed in as part of a
POST or PUT request. Say, for example, that we have an HTML form containing the
elements name, age, and address as follows:

```
<form action="/users" method="POST">
    Name: <input type="text" name="name">
    Age: <input type="text" name="age">
    Address: <input type="text" name="address">
</form>
```

Then, we use the @FormParam annotation as follows:

```
@Path("/users")
public class UserResource {
    @POST
    @Consumes("application/x-www-form-urlencoded")
    public void addUser(@FormParam("name") String name,
        @FormParam("age") int age, @FormParam("address")
            String address) {
    }
}
```

The client connects to our URI through a POST (or PUT) request with the payload
containing the name/value set defined in the form element. When the request
is handled by the framework, we have access to all the values we defined in the
addUser() method, just like we did with the @PathParam annotation.

We now have enough information of all the Jersey annotations we'll need in our web
service, so we move directly to the implementation portion of this chapter.

Web service architecture

The code of this web service is broken down into three layers of abstraction, with each layer corresponding to a package in the code. We have a *web* layer, which contains the Jersey resource classes; a *business* layer, which contains classes that handle the actual storing and retrieving of resources; and a *model* layer, which contains the classes that are stored into our database. Finally, to make the implementation easier, we use Db4o to store users and messages. The full architecture looks as follows:

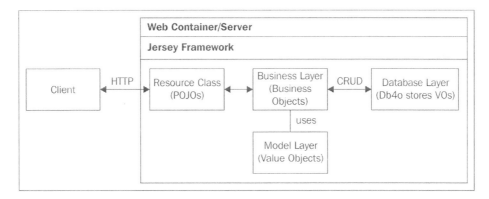

Breaking down the application implementation into layers is a common software engineering practice. With completely separated code layers, classes become components exchanging messages between each other. For example, the resource classes in the *web* layer do nothing but handle communication between the client and the server using the HTTP protocol and then delegate work to the *business* layer. The *business* layer takes in XML representations sent by clients, validates these representations, and converts them to value objects to store into a database.

More importantly for us, this layered approach allows us to interchange the *web* layer with either of the RESTful frameworks we cover in this book and to use the same code base for the *business*, *model*, and *database* packages.

This architecture can be used as a template for more sophisticated web services, by reworking the business and persistence layers. For example, we could use an EJB container for our business layer and a relational database for our data storage layer.

Persistence layer

For the persistence layer we use Db4o, an open source object database engine. It's light and it's easy to use: we store objects and we retrieve objects. Furthermore, Db4o uses a file in the operating system to store data; therefore, we don't require a separate database server running (less moving part equals less chances of introducing bugs).

The following table lists the four basic CRUD functions we'll need for our implementation:

Action	Code sample
Create	```ObjectContainer db = Db4o.openFile("/tmp/db.data");
db.store(new StringBuilder("REST"));
db.close();```
	We open a database connection, and we store the `StringBuilder` object. If the file data `/tmp/db.data` doesn't exist, the Db4o engine creates it.
Read	```ObjectContainer db = Db4o.openFile("/tmp/db.data");
ObjectSet<MessageVO> result =
db.queryByExample(new StringBuilder("REST");
db.close();```
	These statements retrieve the object we just stored.
Delete	```ObjectContainer db = Db4o.openFile("/tmp/db.data");
ObjectSet<MessageVO> result =
db.queryByExample(new String("REST");
if (result.hasNext()) {
StringBuilder tmpString = result.next();
}
db.delete(tmpString);
db.close();```
	To delete a record, we first retrieve it, and then we delete it.
Update	```ObjectContainer db = Db4o.openFile("/tmp/db.data");
ObjectSet<MessageVO> result =
db.queryByExample(new StringBuilder("REST");
if (result.hasNext()) {
StringBuilder tmpString = result.next();
}
tmpString.append("ful Java");
db.store(tmpString);
db.close();```
	To update a record, we retrieve it, we update its content, and then we store it.

RESTful web service implementation with Jersey

In this section we look at the full Jersey implementation of the web service we outlined in Chapter 4. Our API consists of six URIs, and we implement all of them.

The best way to study this chapter is to mentally break down each URI as a use case. Each URI is mapped to a Jersey resource class that is part of the *web* package, as follows:

URI	Jersey resource class
`http://localhost:8080/users`	`UsersResource.class`
`http://localhost:8080/users/{username}`	`UserResource.class`
`http://localhost:8080/messages`	`MessagesResource.class`
`http://localhost:8080/messages/{messageID}`	`MessageResource.class`
`http://localhost:8080/messages/users/{username}`	`UserMessagesResource.class`
`http://localhost:8080/messages/search/{search_item}`	`SearchMessagesResource.class`

These resource classes are the entry point for HTTP requests through specific URIs. From here, we delegate the actual work to utility classes that are part of the *business* package. In the business layer we use value objects or POJO classes (user and message beans), which are part of the *model* package.

To get the most out of this section, download the source code from `http://www.packtpub.com/files/code/6460_Code.zip` (look for `Chapter5`) and follow along with the explanations of each layer.

All resources' implementation use the same pattern: we begin at the web layer and work our way down to the last detail at the business layer.

If you are interested only in what a Jersey resource is or in how to code one, you can just look at the full listing at the beginning of each subsection. The resource classes for each URI are small enough to be typed in a few minutes. Of course, these classes without the code in the rest of the layers make for a dull web service: one that accepts requests, but does nothing.

Application deployment

The directory structure for our application looks as follows:

This screenshot has the full listing of all the files in our web service, including all the libraries required. Again, if you download the source package, everything you need to run the application is in it.

If you only want to deploy a Jersey web service (without Db4o), you only need to make sure the Jersey libraries are part of the **web** project's library folder, and that the web.xml descriptor is modified so that Jersey intercepts all HTTP requests.

The Jersey libraries that are part of the Jersey download are **asm-3.1.jar**, **jersey-core. jar**, **jersey-server.jar**, and **jsr-311-api-1.0.jar**—all must go in the **lib** directory of the web application folder, as shown in the top right-hand side of the screenshot.

The `web.xml` file looks as follows:

```xml
<?xml version="1.0" encoding="UTF-8"?>
<web-app version="2.5"
    xmlns="http://java.sun.com/xml/ns/javaee"
    xmlns:xsi="http://www.w3.org/2001/XMLSchema-instance"
    xsi:schemaLocation="http://java.sun.com/xml/ns/javaee
    http://java.sun.com/xml/ns/javaee/web-app_2_5.xsd">

    <servlet>
        <servlet-name>JerseyWebService</servlet-name>
        <servlet-class>
            com.sun.jersey.spi.container.servlet.ServletContainer
        </servlet-class>
        <load-on-startup>1</load-on-startup>
    </servlet>
    <servlet-mapping>
        <servlet-name>JerseyWebService</servlet-name>
        <url-pattern>/*</url-pattern>
    </servlet-mapping>

    <welcome-file-list>
        <welcome-file>index.jsp</welcome-file>
    </welcome-file-list>
</web-app>
```

Consequently, this is the content of the `web.xml` file of our web service.

URI and resources

Two of the main parts of a web service are resources and URIs. For our Jersey implementation, we map six resource classes with six URIs. We begin with the `/users` URI.

/users

We defined the URI `/users` to accept GET and POST requests. The GET request returns a list of all users, and the POST request creates a new user.

The full listing of the `UsersResource` class looks as follows:

```java
package web;

import javax.ws.rs.GET;
import javax.ws.rs.Path;
import javax.ws.rs.Produces;

import business.UserBO;
```

```
@Path("/users")
public class UsersResource {
    @GET
    @Produces("application/xml")
    public String getXML() {
        return UserBO.getAllXML();
    }

    @GET
    @Produces("application/json")
    public String getJSON() {
        return UserBO.getAllJSON();
    }

    @POST
    @Consumes("application/xml")
    @Produces("application/xml")
    public String createUser(String representation) {
        try {
            return UserBO.create(represen POST request creates a new
                user tation);                   user
        } catch (InvalidXMLException e) {
            throw new WebApplicationException(400);
        } catch (ItemAlreadyExistsException e) {
            throw new WebApplicationException(403);
        }
    }
}
```

HTTP GET

As we discussed earlier, Jersey's annotations let us serve different types of
representations through the same URI. The framework knows how to intercept
HTTP requests and understands what the value of the HTTP *Accept* header means.

When the *Accept* header is not set by the client, the web service will do its best to
send something back. If this happens, the framework will delegate the request to the
first annotated method it finds in the resource class. Consequently, if there is no @GET
annotated method, an exception is thrown by the framework and the client receives
the response as a web server error message.

We provide two type of representations: XML and JSON. Therefore, we have two
methods with the @GET annotation that also use @Produces with a MIME type of
either application/xml or application/json.

XML representation

The request for an XML representation is handled by the `UsersResource.getXML()` method:

```
@GET
@Produces("application/xml")
public String getXML() {
return UserBO.getAllXML();
}
```

And calls the `UserBO.getAllXML()` method, which looks as follows:

```
public static String getAllXML() {
    ObjectContainer db = null;
    try {
        db = Db4o.openFile(Constants.DB_NAME);
        StringBuilder users = new StringBuilder();
        users.append("<users>");

        ObjectSet<UserVO> result = db.queryByExample(UserVO.class);
        users.append("<count>").append(result.size())
            .append("</count>");

        while (result.hasNext()) {
            users.append(result.next().toXML());
        }

        users.append("</users>");

        return users.toString();
    } finally {
        if (db != null) {
            db.close();
        }
    }
}
```

We create the XML representation by getting all the users in the database and then getting each element's XML representation by calling each instance's `toXML()` method, which returns an XML representation.

The line of code where we're telling the Db4o engine to get all records of type `UserVO.class` is this one:

```
ObjectSet<UserVO> result = db.queryByExample(UserVO.class);
```

And the code to get the instance's XML representation is in the method
`UserVO.toXML()`, which looks as follows:

```
public String toXML() {
    StringBuilder xml = new StringBuilder();
    xml.append("<user>");
    xml.append("<username>").append(username).append("</username>");
    xml.append("<password>").append(password).append("</password>");
    xml.append("<link>").append(getLink()).append("</link>");
    xml.append("</user>");

    return xml.toString();
}
```

Note that if there are no users, an empty representation is sent, which looks
as follows:

```
<users>
<count>0</count>
</users>
```

JSON representation

Subsequently, we serve a JSON representation of all users with this method:

```
@GET
@Produces("application/json")
public String getJSON() {
    return UserBO.getAllJSON();
}
```

And we delegate the work to the method `UserBO.getJSON()`, which looks
as follows:

```
public static String getAllJSON() {
    ObjectContainer db = null;
    try {
        db = Db4o.openFile(Constants.DB_NAME);
        StringBuilder users = new StringBuilder();
        ObjectSet<UserVO> result = db
            .queryByExample(UserVO.class);
        users.append("{\"users-result\":{\"count\":\"")
            .append(result.size()).append("\", \"users\":[");
        while (result.hasNext()) {
            users.append(result.next().toJSON());

            if (result.hasNext()) {
```

```
            users.append(",");
        }
    }
    users.append("]}}");
    return users.toString();
} finally {
    if (db != null) {
        db.close();
    }
}
}
```

We need to separate each record in the JSON representation, so we must append the , character between each element. Other than that, the coding pattern is the same as the one we use when we get the XML representation: we loop through the results and call each of the toJSON() method of the UserVO instance.

Finally, the code for the UserVO.toJSON() method looks as follows:

```
public String toJSON() {
    StringBuilder json = new StringBuilder();
    json.append("{\"user\":{\"username\":\"")
        .append(username).append("\", \"password\":\"")
        .append(password).append("\", \"link\":\"")
        .append(getLink()).append("\"}}");
    return json.toString();
}
```

If there are no users, the empty JSON structure looks as follows:

```
{"users-result":{"count":"0", "users":[]}}
```

When we outlined the steps of RESTful web service design, we said that a well-behaved service provides multiple representations of the same resource.

As our application is a well-behaved web service, we provide XML and JSON representations for all of our resources.

HTTP POST

Creating a new user is handled by the `UsersResource.createUser()` method, which looks as follows:

```
@POST
@Consumes("application/xml")
@Produces("application/xml")
public String createUser(String representation) {
    try {
        return UserBO.create(representation);
    } catch (InvalidXMLException e) {
        throw new WebApplicationException(400);
    } catch (ItemAlreadyExistsException e) {
        throw new WebApplicationException(403);
    }
}
```

First, we store the resource's representation that comes in as an XML payload of the POST request. Then we return back an XML representation of the resource we just stored. If there are any errors, we check for thrown exceptions and re-throw them as web exceptions back to the client.

Now, the details: we use the annotation `@Consumes("application/xml")` to consume the appropriate format of the payload. The payload of the POST request is stored in the String object `representation`. The value of this object is the XML representation of a user.

We delegate the actual resource creation to the `UserBO.create()` method, which looks as follows:

```
public static String create(String xml) throws InvalidXMLException,
    ItemAlreadyExistsException {
    ObjectContainer db = null;
    try {
        db = Db4o.openFile(Constants.DB_NAME);
        UserVO userVO = XMLUtil.getUserVOFromXML(xml);
        if (userVO != null) {
            // Check if user exists in our DB: if not, create;
            // else, throw exception
            if (query(db, userVO.getUsername()) == null) {
                db.store(userVO);

                return userVO.toXML();
            } else {
                throw new ItemAlreadyExistsException();
            }
```

```
        } else {
            throw new InvalidXMLException();
        }
    } finally {
        if (db != null) {
            db.close();
        }
    }
}
```

This method opens our database for insertion and gets a user value object from the XML sent in. Before storing the record, the XML must be validated—if the XML is not valid, an InvalidXMLException exception is thrown. Once the XML representation has been validated, we need to check that the user doesn't already exist—if a user with the same identifier already exists, an ItemAlreadyExistsException exception is thrown. Again, only when the XML representation has been validated and only when we have checked that a user with the same username doesn't exist, we store the user value object.

Validating the XML representation is done with the call to the method XMLUtil.getUserVOFromXML(). The listing for this method looks as follows:

```
public static UserVO getUserVOFromXML(String xml) {
    Document doc = getDocument(xml);
    if (doc != null) {
        if(validateUserXML(doc)) {
            // XML is valid, just get the values from the DOM
            return new UserVO(getValue((Element)
                doc.getElementsByTagName("user").item(0),
                "username"), getValue((Element)
                doc.getElementsByTagName("user")
                .item(0), "password"));
        }
    }
    return null;
}
```

From our specification document, we know that a valid user XML representation looks as follows:

```
<user>
  <username>username</username>
  <password>password</password>
  <link></link>
</user>
```

We validate the XML representation with the method `XMLUtil.validateUserXML()`:

```
private static boolean validateUserXML(Document doc) {
    NodeList nodeList = null;

    // Check the elements and values exist
    nodeList = doc.getElementsByTagName("user");
    if (nodeList.getLength() != 1) {
        return false;
    }
    // Check that email element exists
    nodeList = doc.getElementsByTagName("username");
    if (nodeList.getLength() != 1) {
        return false;
    }
    // Check that value is not null or empty
    String username = getValue((Element) doc
        .getElementsByTagName("user").item(0), "username");
    if (username == null || username.isEmpty()) {
        return false;
    }
    // Check that email element exists
    nodeList = doc.getElementsByTagName("password");
    if (nodeList.getLength() != 1) {
        return false;
    }
    // Check that value is not null or empty
    String password = getValue((Element) doc
        .getElementsByTagName("user").item(0), "password");
    if (password == null || password.isEmpty()) {
        return false;
    }
    return true;
}
```

This is a simple validation routine: all we need to do is to check that all the nodes of the XML structure exist and that all the values of the nodes are not `null` or empty (this is the brute force approach, but we could use an XML schema to do the validation; adding this type of validation, however, adds more code to our implementation).

We previously said that once the user value object has been stored, we return the XML representation back to the client. The annotation `@Produces("application/xml")` makes sure to set the appropriate MIME type for the response stream. The following line in the `UsersResource.createUser()` method takes care of sending the representation back to the client:

```
return UserBO.create(representation);
```

The return value is also tied with the signature of the annotated method. For instance, the signature of the `UsersResource.createUser()` method returns a String object, but it could just as easily return a different type of object that must match the value of the `@Produces` annotation.

Lastly, the `UserResource.createUser()` method can throw two types of exceptions when errors are encountered. For example, the `UserBO.create()` method can throw either `ItemAlreadyExistsException` or `InvalidXMLException`. The exceptions are then caught at the web layer and are re-thrown as `WebApplicationException` exceptions, with appropriate HTTP error codes, as follows:

```
try {
    return UserBO.create(representation);
} catch (InvalidXMLException e) {
    throw new WebApplicationException(400);
} catch (ItemAlreadyExistsException e) {
    throw new WebApplicationException(403);
}
```

/users/{username}

With this URI we retrieve, update, and delete user records. The full listing for the `UserResource` class looks as follows:

```
package web;

import javax.ws.rs.Consumes;
import javax.ws.rs.DELETE;
import javax.ws.rs.GET;
import javax.ws.rs.PUT;
import javax.ws.rs.Path;
import javax.ws.rs.PathParam;
import javax.ws.rs.Produces;
import javax.ws.rs.WebApplicationException;

import business.UserBO;
import exception.InvalidXMLException;
import exception.ItemAlreadyExistsException;
import exception.ItemNotFoundException;
```

```
@Path("/users/{username}")
public class UserResource {
    @GET
    @Produces("application/xml")
    public String getXML(@PathParam("username") String username) {
        String xml = UserBO.getXML(username);
        if (xml != null) {
            return xml;
        } else {
            throw new WebApplicationException(404);
        }
    }

    @GET
    @Produces("application/json")
    public String getJSON(@PathParam("username") String username) {
        String json = UserBO.getJSON(username);
        if (json != null) {
            return json;
        } else {
            throw new WebApplicationException(404);
        }
    }

    @PUT
    @Consumes("application/xml")
    @Produces("application/xml")
    public String updateUser(@PathParam("username") username,
        String representation) {
        try {
            return UserBO.update(representation);
        } catch (InvalidXMLException e) {
            throw new WebApplicationException(400);
        } catch (ItemNotFoundException e) {
            throw new WebApplicationException(404);
        }
    }

    @DELETE
    public void deleteUser(@PathParam("username") String username) {
        try {
            UserBO.delete(username);
        } catch (ItemNotFoundException e) {
            throw new WebApplicationException(404);
        }
    }
}
```

HTTP GET

Similar to our `UsersResource` class, we provide XML and JSON representations of the same resource.

XML representation

We serve an XML representation with the method call:

```
@GET
@Produces("application/xml")
public String getXML(@PathParam("username") String username) {
    String xml = UserBO.getXML(username);
    if (xml != null) {
        return xml;
    } else {
        throw new WebApplicationException(404);
    }
}
```

Again, this method handles a GET request because of the `@GET` annotation and returns an XML representation because of the `@Produces("application/xml")` annotation. In addition, the `@PathParam("username")` annotation together with the String object `username` gives us access to the variable defined in `@Path` `("/users/{username}")`.

And we delegate the work to the `UserBO.getXML()` method, which looks as follows:

```
public static String getXML(String username) {
    UserVO userVO = query(username);
    return (userVO != null) ? userVO.toXML() : null;
}
```

We first get an instance of the stored user with the `UserBO.query()` method, which looks as follows:

```
protected static UserVO query(String username) {
    ObjectContainer db = null;
    try {
        db = Db4o.openFile(Constants.DB_NAME);
        ObjectSet<UserVO> result = db.queryByExample(new
            UserVO(username));
        if (result.hasNext()) {
            return result.next();
        } else {
            return null;
        }
    } finally {
```

```
            if (db != null) {
                db.close();
            }
        }
    }
```

JSON representation

We serve a JSON representation with the method call:

```
@GET
@Produces("application/json")
public String getJSON(@PathParam("username") String username) {
    String json = UserBO.getJSON(username);
    if (json != null) {
        return json;
    } else {
        throw new WebApplicationException(404);
    }
}
```

In this method, we call our business layer to retrieve the JSON representation of the resource with the identifier username. The UserBO.getJSON() method looks as follows:

```
public static String getJSON(String username) {
    UserVO userVO = query(username);
    return (userVO != null) ? userVO.toJSON() : null;
}
```

HTTP PUT

Our web service allows users to update their account password. At this point we know the user's identifier, the value we get from the URI with the @PathParam annotation. The listing for the method handling a PUT request looks as follows:

```
@PUT
@Consumes("application/xml")
@Produces("application/xml")
public String updateUser(@PathParam("username") String username,
    String representation) {
    try {
        return UserBO.update(representation);
    } catch (InvalidXMLException e) {
```

```
            throw new WebApplicationException(400);
    } catch (ItemNotFoundException e) {
            throw new WebApplicationException(404);
    }
}
```

This method delegates the record updating to `UserBO.update()`, which looks as follows:

```
public static String update(String xml) throws InvalidXMLException,
    ItemNotFoundException {
    ObjectContainer db = null;
    try {
            db = Db4o.openFile(Constants.DB_NAME);
            UserVO userVO = XMLUtil.getUserVOFromXML(xml);
            if (userVO != null) {
            // Check that user exists in our DB: if so, update;
            // else, throw exception
            UserVO tmpUser = query(db, userVO.getUsername());
            if (tmpUser != null) {
                // We only let the user update the password
                tmpUser.setPassword(userVO.getPassword());
                db.store(tmpUser);
                return tmpUser.toXML();
            } else {
                throw new ItemNotFoundException();
            }
        } else {
            throw new InvalidXMLException();
        }
    } finally {
        if (db != null) {
            db.close();
        }
    }
}
```

We first validate the XML representation sent by the client. If the XML is valid, we retrieve the record for user in the representation. We then update the password field of the resource and we store the updated resource; once the representation is stored, we return it back to the caller as an XML structure.

HTTP DELETE

We delete user resources using the same URI as the rest of our earlier requests, but the HTTP method is now DELETE. The method for deleting a resource looks as follows:

```
@DELETE
public void deleteUser(@PathParam("username") String username) {
    try {
        UserBO.delete(username);
    } catch (ItemNotFoundException e) {
        throw new WebApplicationException(404);
    }
}
```

This method call delegates the deleting to the method `UserBO.delete()`, which looks as follows:

```
public static void delete(String username)
    throws ItemNotFoundException {
    ObjectContainer db = null;
    try {
        db = Db4o.openFile(Constants.DB_NAME);
        // Check that user for username exists
        UserVO userVO = query(db, username);
        if (userVO != null) {
            db.delete(userVO);
        } else {
            throw new ItemNotFoundException();
        }
    } finally {
        if (db != null) {
            db.close();
        }
    }
}
```

We first check that the resource actually exists. If it does, we delete it; if it doesn't we throw an `ItemNotFoundException` exception that is re-thrown by `UserResource.deleteUser()` as a `WebApplicationException` exception.

/messages

With this URI we create messages and retrieve representations of messages.
The MessagesResource class looks as follows:

```java
package web;

import javax.ws.rs.GET;
import javax.ws.rs.Path;
import javax.ws.rs.Produces;

import business.MessageBO;

@Path("/messages")
public class MessagesResource {
    @GET
    @Produces("application/xml")
    public String getXML() {
        return MessageBO.getAllXML();
    }

    @GET
    @Produces("application/json")
    public String getJSON() {
        return MessageBO.getAllJSON();
    }

    @POST
    @Consumes("application/xml")
    @Produces("application/xml")
    public String createMessage(String representation) {
        try {
            return MessageBO.create(representation);
        } catch (InvalidXMLException e) {
            throw new WebApplicationException(400);
        } catch (UserNotFoundException e) {
            throw new WebApplicationException(403);
        }
    }
}
```

HTTP GET

We provide XML or JSON representation of all messages.

XML representation

We serve an XML representation with the method:

```
@GET
@Produces("application/xml")
public String getXML() {
    return MessageBO.getAllXML();
}
```

This call delegates the work to the method `MessageBO.getAllXML()`, which looks as follows:

```
public static String getAllXML() {
    ObjectContainer db = null;
    try {
        db = Db4o.openFile(Constants.DB_NAME);
        StringBuilder users = new StringBuilder();
        users.append("<messages>");

        ObjectSet<MessageVO> result = db
            .queryByExample(MessageVO.class);
        users.append("<count>").append(result.size())
            .append("</count>");

        while (result.hasNext()) {
            users.append(result.next().toXML());
        }
        users.append("</messages>");

        return users.toString();
    } finally {
        if (db != null) {
            db.close();
        }
    }
}
```

We create the XML representation by looping through each message and calling the instance's `MessageVO.toXML()` method, which looks as follows:

```
public String toXML() {
    StringBuilder xml = new StringBuilder();
    xml.append("<message>");
```

```
xml.append("<messageID>").append(messageID)
    .append("</messageID>");
xml.append("<content>").append(content).append("</content>");
xml.append("<link>").append(getLink()).append("</link>");
xml.append(userVO.toXML());
xml.append("</message>");

return xml.toString();
```
}

Note that we also call the `UserVO.toXML()` method of the embedded user in the message's instance. This call gets the XML representation of the user who posted the message (as per our requirements).

JSON representation

We serve a JSON representation with the method:

```
@GET
@Produces("application/json")
public String getJSON() {
    return MessageBO.getAllJSON();
}
```

To get a JSON representation we use the method call `MessageBO.getAllJSON()`, which looks as follows:

```
public static String getAllJSON() {
    ObjectContainer db = null;
    try {
        db = Db4o.openFile(Constants.DB_NAME);
        // Refer to Chapter 4 for the specific structure
        StringBuilder messages = new StringBuilder();

        ObjectSet<MessageVO> result = db
            .queryByExample(MessageVO.class);
        messages.append("{\"messages-result\":{\"count\":\"")
            .append(result.size()).append("\", \"messages\":[");
        while (result.hasNext()) {
            messages.append(result.next().toJSON());

            if (result.hasNext()) {
                messages.append(",");
            }
        }

        messages.append("]}}");
```

```
        return messages.toString();
    } finally {
        if (db != null) {
            db.close();
        }
    }
}
```

This code looks similar to the code we used for getting the XML representation, except that we are creating a JSON representation, and therefore we call the toJSON() method of each message's instance, which looks as follows:

```
public String toJSON() {
    StringBuilder json = new StringBuilder();

    json.append("{\"message\":{\"messageID\":\"")
        .append(messageID).append("\", \"content\":\"")
        .append(content).append("\", \"link\":\"")
        .append(getLink()).append("\", \"")
        .append(userVO.toJSON()).append("}}");

    return json.toString();
}
```

Again, we also need to call the user's instance toJSON() method to get the appropriate user representation that is part of the message.

HTTP POST

We create a message with the following method:

```
@POST
@Consumes("application/xml")
@Produces("application/xml")
public String createMessage(String representation) {
    try {
        return MessageBO.create(representation);
    } catch (InvalidXMLException e) {
        throw new WebApplicationException(400);
    } catch (UserNotFoundException e) {
        throw new WebApplicationException(403);
    }
}
```

This method delegates the creation of a message to the method MessageBO.create(), which looks as follows:

```
public static String create(String xml)
    throws InvalidXMLException, UserNotFoundException {
    ObjectContainer db = null;
```

```
    try {
        db = Db4o.openFile(Constants.DB_NAME);
        MessageVO messageVO = XMLUtil.getMessageVOFromXML(xml);
        if (messageVO != null) {
        // Add message only if user is registered
        if (UserBO.query(db, messageVO.getUserVO().getUsername(),
            messageVO.getUserVO().getPassword()) != null) {
            db.store(messageVO);

            return messageVO.toXML();
        } else {
            throw new UserNotFoundException();
                }
        } else {
            throw new InvalidXMLException();
        }
    } finally {
        if (db != null) {
            db.close();
        }
    }
}
```

This call validates the XML structure and stores the record in our database. If the XML is not valid or the user within the XML doesn't exist, the appropriate exception is thrown and, finally, it returns the XML representation of the stored record back to the client.

From our specification in Chapter 4, *RESTful Web Services Design*, we know that a valid XML representation for a message looks as follows:

```
<message>
    <messageID></messageID>
    <content></content>
    <link></link>
    <user>
        <username></username>
        <password></password>
        <link></link>
    </user>
</message>
```

Therefore, we validate a message representation with the method XMLUtil.getMessageVOFromXML(), which looks as follows:

```
public static MessageVO getMessageVOFromXML(String xml) {
    Document doc = getDocument(xml);
    if (doc != null) {
        if (validateMessageXML(doc, xml)) {
```

```
                    // XML is valid, just get the values from the DOM
                    UserVO userVO = new UserVO(getValue((Element)
                        doc.getElementsByTagName("user").item(0),
                        "username"), getValue((Element) doc
                        .getElementsByTagName("user").item(0), "password"));
                    return new MessageVO(getValue((Element) doc
                        .getElementsByTagName("message").item(0),
                        "content"), userVO);
                }
            }

        return null;
    }
```

Validating the XML representation sent by the client is done in the method, `XMLUtil.validateMessageXML()`, which looks as follows:

```
    private static boolean validateMessageXML(Document doc, String xml) {
        NodeList nodeList = null;

        // Check the elements and values exist
        nodeList = doc.getElementsByTagName("message");
        if (nodeList.getLength() != 1) {
            return false;
        }
        // Check that email element exists
            nodeList = doc.getElementsByTagName("content");
        if (nodeList.getLength() != 1) {
            return false;
        }
        // Check that value is not null or empty
            String content = getValue((Element) doc
                .getElementsByTagName("message").item(0), "content");
        if (content == null || content.isEmpty()) {
            return false;
        }
        // Validate that user is part of the message XML
        return validateUserXML(doc);
    }
```

Validating the XML for a message takes a few more steps than validating a user, because of the user's XML representation embedded within the message. Nonetheless, we use the same idea of checking for the existence of the nodes and the value of the nodes, and we call the XMLUtil.validateUserXML() method (which we already saw for the user). If all the required nodes exist and have valid values, we return true; otherwise, false.

Finally, when the XML for the message is valid, we need to instantiate a UserVO object from the message's XML structure, because a message record must have a valid user. We instantiate a UserVO object by getting the values directly from the DOM we created out of the XML passed by the client, as follows:

```
UserVO userVO = new UserVO(getValue((Element) doc
    .getElementsByTagName("user").item(0), "username"),
        getValue((Element) doc.getElementsByTagName("user")
            .item(0), "password"));
```

/messages/{messageID}

The Jersey resource for each message follows the same coding pattern we used for /users/{username}. However, for a message, we don't support the HTTP PUT method call, as we don't allow updates to messages.

The full listing for the MessageResource class looks as follows:

```
package web;

import javax.ws.rs.Consumes;
import javax.ws.rs.DELETE;
import javax.ws.rs.GET;
import javax.ws.rs.POST;
import javax.ws.rs.Path;
import javax.ws.rs.PathParam;
import javax.ws.rs.Produces;
import javax.ws.rs.WebApplicationException;

import business.MessageBO;
import exception.InvalidXMLException;
import exception.ItemNotFoundException;
import exception.UserNotFoundException;

@Path("/messages/{messageID}")
public class MessageResource {
    @GET
    @Produces("application/xml")
    public String getXML(@PathParam("messageID") String messageID) {
        String xml = MessageBO.getXML(messageID);
```

```
            if (xml != null) {
                return xml;
            } else {
                throw new WebApplicationException(404);
            }
        }

        @GET
        @Produces("application/json")
        public String getJSON(@PathParam("messageID") String messageID) {
            String json = MessageBO.getJSON(messageID);
            if (json != null) {
                return json;
            } else {
                throw new WebApplicationException(404);
            }
        }

        @DELETE
        public void deleteMessage(@PathParam("messageID")
            String messageID) {
            try {
                MessageBO.delete(messageID);
            } catch (ItemNotFoundException e) {
                throw new WebApplicationException(404);
            }
        }
    }
}
```

HTTP GET

We provide XML and JSON representations, same as we did for users. We also have
the same pattern of using the annotations @GET and @Produces.

XML representation

We serve an XML representation with the method:

```
@GET
@Produces("application/xml")
public String getXML(@PathParam("messageID") String messageID) {
    String xml = MessageBO.getXML(messageID);
    if (xml != null) {
        return xml;
    } else {
        throw new WebApplicationException(404);
    }
}
```

And we delegate the work to the method `MessageBO.getXML()`, which looks as follows:

```
public static String getXML(String messageID) {
    MessageVO messageVO = queryMessage(messageID);
    return (messageVO != null) ? messageVO.toXML() : null;
}
```

To retrieve the message value object from our database, we make a call to the `MessageBO.queryMessage()` method, which looks as follows:

```
private static MessageVO queryMessage(String messageID) {
    ObjectContainer db = null;
    try {
        db = Db4o.openFile(Constants.DB_NAME);
        ObjectSet<MessageVO> result = db
            .queryByExample(new MessageVO(messageID));
        if (result.hasNext()) {
            return result.next();
        } else {
            return null;
        }
    } finally {
        if (db != null) {
            db.close();
        }
    }
}
```

It's the same technique we used for retrieving users: we connect to the database and retrieve the message that matches the unique identifier `messageID`. Once the message has been retrieved, we return the XML structure of the value object by calling the `toXML()` method of the `MessageVO` instance.

JSON representation

We serve a JSON representation with the method:

```
@GET
@Produces("application/json")
public String getJSON(@PathParam("messageID") String messageID) {
    String json = MessageBO.getJSON(messageID);
    if (json != null) {
        return json;
    } else {
        throw new WebApplicationException(404);
    }
}
```

And we delegate the work to the `MessageBO.getJSON()` method, which looks as follows:

```
public static String getJSON(String messageID) {
    MessageVO messageVO = queryMessage(messageID);
    return (messageVO != null) ? messageVO.toJSON() : null;
}
```

This is the same idea as the XML structure, except that instead of calling `toXML()` we call the `toJSON()` method of the `MessageVO` instance.

HTTP DELETE

Deleting a message is done through the `MessageResrouce.deleteMessage()` method, which looks as follows:

```
@DELETE
public void deleteMessage(@PathParam("messageID") String messageID) {
    try {
        MessageBO.delete(messageID);
    } catch (ItemNotFoundException e) {
        throw new WebApplicationException(404);
    }
}
```

This method delegates the deleting to the `MessageBO.delete()` method, which looks as follows:

```
public static void delete(String messageID) throws
        ItemNotFoundException {
    ObjectContainer db = null;
    try {
        db = Db4o.openFile(Constants.DB_NAME);
        // Check that message for messageID exists
        MessageVO messageVO = queryMessage(db, messageID);
        if (messageVO != null) {
            db.delete(messageVO);
        } else {
            throw new ItemNotFoundException();
        }
    } finally {
        if (db != null) {
            db.close();
        }
    }
}
```

We first check that the message with the identifier `messageID` exists, and then we delete it.

/messages/users/{username}

This URI is telling the service to retrieve all the messages that have been added by a user with identifier `username`.

The full listing for the `UserMessagesResource` class looks as follows:

```
package web;

import javax.ws.rs.GET;
import javax.ws.rs.Path;
import javax.ws.rs.PathParam;
import javax.ws.rs.Produces;

import business.MessageBO;

@Path("/messages/users/{username}")
public class UserMessagesResource {
    @GET
    @Produces("application/xml")
    public String getXML(@PathParam("username") String username) {
        return MessageBO.getAllXMLForUser(username);
    }

    @GET
    @Produces("application/json")
    public String getJSON(@PathParam("username") String username) {
        return MessageBO.getAllJSONForUser(username);
    }
}
```

HTTP GET

As per our specification, we provide XML and JSON representations.

XML representation

We serve an XML representation with the method:

```
@GET
@Produces("application/xml")
public String getXML(@PathParam("username") String username) {
    return MessageBO.getAllXMLForUser(username);
}
```

And we delegate the work to the `MessageBO.getAllXMLForUser()` method, which looks as follows:

```
public static String getAllXMLForUser(String username) {
    return getAllXMLStructure(getAllForUser(username));
}
```

We already know how to create an XML representation for a list of messages, but we don't know how to search for messages that have been posted by a specific user. Therefore, we introduce the method `MessageBO.getAllForUser()`, which looks as follows:

```
private static List<MessageVO> getAllForUser(final String username) {
    ObjectContainer db = null;
    List<MessageVO> list = null;

    try {
        db = Db4o.openFile(Constants.DB_NAME);

        // Check that user exists
        final UserVO userVO = UserBO.query(db, username);
        if (userVO == null) {
            return new ArrayList<MessageVO>();
        }

        list = db.query(new Predicate<MessageVO>() {
            public boolean match(MessageVO messageVO) {
            return (messageVO.getUserVO().getUsername()
                .equals(username));
            }
        });

        ArrayList<MessageVO> newList = new ArrayList<MessageVO>();
        for (MessageVO vo : list) {
            newList.add(vo);
        }

        return (list == null) ? new ArrayList<MessageVO>() : newList;
    } finally {
        if (db != null) {
            db.close();
        }
    }
}
```

First, we make sure that the user we have been given is valid; then we retrieve all the messages posted by the user we've just validated. We retrieve the records saved by a particular user with these statements:

```
list = db.query(new Predicate<MessageVO>() {
    public boolean match(MessageVO messageVO) {
        return (messageVO.getUserVO().getUsername()
            .equals(username));
    }
});
```

JSON representation

We serve a JSON representation with the method:

```
@GET
@Produces("application/json")
public String getJSON(@PathParam("username") String username) {
    return MessageBO.getAllJSONForUser(username);
}
```

And we delegate the work to the `MessageBO.getAllJSONForUser()` method, which looks as follows:

```
public static String getAllJSONForUser(String username) {
    return getAllJSONStructure(getAllForUser(username));
}
```

We've already seen how to retrieve messages for a particular user and also how to create a JSON representation for a list of messages (code reuse at its best).

/messages/search/{search_item}

In Chapter 4, we talked about URIs executing logic on the web service. By now, we should know how to implement this resource, because it's similar to the one we just worked through (getting messages for a particular user). The difference here is that we're searching for messages that contain a particular string.

The full listing for the `SearchMessagesResource` class looks as follows:

```
package web;

import javax.ws.rs.GET;
import javax.ws.rs.Path;
import javax.ws.rs.PathParam;
import javax.ws.rs.Produces;

import business.MessageBO;
```

```
@Path("/messages/search/{search_item}")
public class SearchMessagesResource {
    @GET
    @Produces("application/xml")
    public String searchXML(@PathParam("search_item")
        String search_item) {
        return MessageBO.searchAllXML(search_item);
    }

    @GET
    @Produces("application/json")
    public String searchJSON(@PathParam("search_item")
        String search_item) {
        return MessageBO.searchAllJSON(search_item);
    }
}
```

HTTP GET

We provide XML and JSON representations.

XML representation

We serve an XML representation with the method:

```
@GET
@Produces("application/xml")
public String searchXML(@PathParam("search_item") String search_item)
{
    return MessageBO.searchAllXML(search_item);
}
```

And we delegate the work to the method `MessageBO.searchAllXML()`, which looks as follows:

```
public static String searchAllXML(String search_item) {
    return getAllXMLStructure(searchMessages(search_item));
}
```

We already know how to create an XML representation of a list of messages, so we won't list the code again. The only thing we don't know yet is how to search for messages that contain the string `search_item`. We execute this search in the `MessageBO.searchMessages()` method, which looks as follows:

```
private static List<MessageVO> searchMessages(final String
    search_item) {
    ObjectContainer db = null;
```

```
        List<MessageVO> list = null;
        try {
            db = Db4o.openFile(Constants.DB_NAME);
            list = db.query(new Predicate<MessageVO>() {
                public boolean match(MessageVO messageVO) {
                    return messageVO.getContent().contains(search_item);
                }
            });
            ArrayList<MessageVO> newList = new ArrayList<MessageVO>();
            for (MessageVO vo : list) {
                newList.add(vo);
            }

            return (list == null) ? new ArrayList<MessageVO>() : newList;
        } finally {
            if (db != null) {
                db.close();
            }
        }
    }
```

We use Db4o's searching capabilities with the following statements (it's the same idea that we used for retrieving messages posted by a particular user):

```
list = db.query(new Predicate<MessageVO>() {
    public boolean match(MessageVO messageVO) {
        return messageVO.getContent().contains(search_item);
    }
});
```

This code limits the result to only messages for which the content field contains the string search_item.

JSON representation

We serve a JSON representation with the method:

```
@GET
@Produces("application/json")
public String searchJSON(@PathParam("search_item")
    String search_item) {
    return MessageBO.searchAllJSON(search_item);
}
```

And we delegate the work to the `MessageBO.searchAllJSON()` method, which looks as follows:

```
public static String searchAllJSON(String search_item) {
    return getAllJSONStructure(searchMessages(search_item));
}
```

The description of all the code used in this method has already been covered.

Using this RESTful web service

We are now ready to use this web service. If you have downloaded the code, deploy the application to your local web server to play around with it. To test the API, you can either use the Swing client we developed in Chapter 2, *Accessing RESTful Services – Part 1* (in fact, this is how I fully tested all the URIs), or you can develop an HTML application using the techniques we covered in Chapter 3, *Accessing RESTful Services – Part 2* (this would make for a nice and quick programming exercise). And if you are feeling adventurous, you can add a couple of more URIs and convert this application to a Twitter clone: all we need now is the idea of registered users following registered users, which is not too hard to code.

Summary

With the use of annotations, Jersey's implementation of the JAX-RS API provides a simple development model for web service programming. In this chapter, we covered the entire framework, and developed a non-trivial RESTful web service. What's more, we have taken a set of specification (written in Chapter 4, *RESTful Web Services Design*) and connected the always-complicated step of creating software from software requirements.

Software frameworks such as Jersey are not complete solutions until we provide the context and solve a specific problem. Our approach has been to separate layers of abstraction to fully understand how the component nature of Object Oriented Development fits within modern software frameworks.

Finally, with Jersey covered, we move onto our next framework: the open source Restlet framework.

6
The Restlet Framework

In this chapter we study the Restlet framework, and implement our sample web service in two of the framework's latest versions.

The Restlet framework was among the first Java frameworks developed that adhered to the REST philosophy. There were others, but Restlet found a solid following because of its ease of use and 100% Java compatibility. It's developed by a French web consulting firm, and the framework is now an open source project. At the time of this writing, the official released version is Restlet 1.1, with Restlet 2.0 still under development.

At the end of this chapter, you'll have enough information to implement web services in both versions. And if you already have a Restlet 1.1 web service and want to use the newest release, you'll be able to compare where the differences are and begin refactoring immediately.

Getting the tools

Even though, everything you need to run the web service is already in the source package of the book, you can download the tools we use, as per the following table:

Software	Web location
Java JDK	http://java.sun.com/
Apache Tomcat	http://tomcat.apache.org/download-60.cgi
Db4o	http://developer.db4o.com/files/default.aspx
Restlet Framework 1.1 and 2.0	http://www.restlet.org/downloads/

Install the latest Java JDK together with the latest version of Tomcat, if you haven't done so. Download and install Db4o and Restlet and note the location of the installs.

Restlet

Restlet provides REST support using its standalone application architecture and a web container module that plugs into any Java web container as a Servlet extension. For the purpose of this chapter, we only look at the Java web container module, which we configure using the file web.xml of a Java web application.

Our implementation architecture for both Restlet versions 1.1 and 2.0 looks as follows:

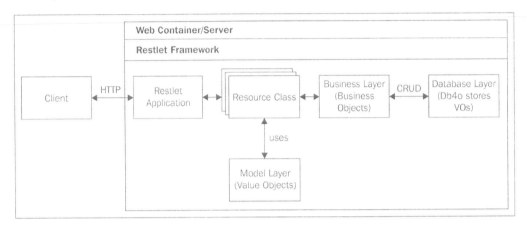

As with any web service, clients and servers exchange representations through predefined URIs. In a Restlet solution, the web server directs requests to a Restlet layer (a Servlet). In this layer, a Restlet application delegates HTTP requests to specific Restlet resources. In the resource classes, as per our implementation architecture, we delegate the actual work to a business layer that takes care of serializing users and messages to a Db4o database.

As per our requirements in Chapter 4, we need to implement six URIs. These URIs are mapped to Restlet resources, as described in the following table:

URI	Restlet resource class
http://localhost:8080/users	UsersResource.class
http://localhost:8080/users/{username}	UserResource.class
http://localhost:8080/messages	MessagesResource.class
http://localhost:8080/messages/{messageID}	MessageResource.class
http://localhost:8080/messages/users/{username}	UserMessagesResource.class
http://localhost:8080/messages/search/{search_item}	SearchMessagesResource.class

We implement the full API with Restlet 1.1 and 2.0. The implementation pattern looks the same for both versions, and we use the same resource names. However, both implementations live under different web application contexts.

To get the most out of this chapter, download the source code from `http://www.packtpub.com/files/code/6460_Code.zip` (look for `Chapter6`) and follow the explanations of the web layer. When you download the code, you'll see two web projects: one corresponding to version 1.1; the other, to version 2.0.

If you download the source code, you can deploy both versions (1.1 and 2.0) to your web container, as each application lives in its own web context. For example, assuming you're running your web container in your local machine, you have deployed both web applications, and you want to access the list of users in your database, you access version 1.1 with `http://localhost:8080/RESTfulJava_Chapter6v1.1/users` and version 2.0 with `http://localhost:8080/RESTfulJava_Chapter6v2.0/users`.

As explained in Chapter 5, we broke down the code into multiple layers so that we could reuse a large portion of the *Business Layer* implementation. Therefore, we won't go into the details of how to store, retrieve, update, or delete user and message resources, because it has already been covered (if you haven't read Chapter 5, you could look at the *Persistence Layer* section and quickly go through the code details; however, it's not necessary for you to have read Chapter 5 to follow along).

Restlet 1.1

The implementation architecture diagram already gives an idea of what we need to implement in the web layer. Specifically, we need to code a Restlet application that maps URIs to Restlet resources, which are the last recipients of HTTP requests. However, before we look at our implementation, we need to first understand what a Restlet application is, and second, we need to understand how HTTP requests are handled by Restlet resources.

Restlet application and URI mappings

In version 1.1, URI mapping is done in an application class that extends `org.restlet.Application`. In our extending class, we override the `createRoot()` method, which attaches resources to an `org.restlet.Router` class. A complete, yet arbitrary, Restlet application class looks as follows:

```
public class RESTfulJavaWebService extends Application {
    public RESTfulJavaWebService(Context parentContext) {
        super(parentContext);
```

```
    }

    @Override
    public synchronized Restlet createRoot() {
        Router router = new Router(getContext());

        // Define routers for users
        router.attach("/users", UsersResource.class);
        router.attach("/users/{usename}", UserResource.class);

    }
}
```

This class maps two URIs to two corresponding resource classes: /users to UsersResources.class and /users/{username} to UserResource.class.

 This style of resource mapping is not the only way of handling HTTP requests. We could write inline org.restlet.Restlet handlers, but then maintenance of code may become cumbersome. Mapping URIs to encapsulated Restlet resources makes development and maintenance easier in the long run.

Handling HTTP requests

Requests are handled by Restlet resource classes that extend org.restlet. resource.Resource. Version 1.1 of the Restlet framework relies on method overriding to support the typical HTTP request method types (GET, POST, PUT, and DELETE). What's more, we need to specifically tell the framework of the requests it needs to handle by overriding all, or a set, of the four methods: allowGet(), allowPost(), allowPut(), and allowDelete().

HTTP GET and content negotiation (HTTP Accept header)

Before a Restlet resource is able to handle GET requests, we need to specifically tell it that GET requests are allowed. We do this by overriding the allowGet() method to return a Boolean value of true. With the resource now able to handle GET requests, we have to override the represent() method. In code, overriding these two methods looks as follows:

```
public class AResource extends Resource {
    @Override
    public boolean allowGet() {
```

```
        return true;
    }

    @Override
    public Representation represent(Variant variant) throws
    ResourceException {
        // Do something...
    }
}
```

When a URI has a variable, as we do in our requirements with /users/{username}, where {username} is the runtime variable, we access the variable's value as follows:

```
    @Override
    public Representation represent(Variant variant) throws
    ResourceException {
        String username = (String) getRequest().getAttributes()
            .get("username");
    }
```

The variable is part of the URI and its reference is part of the request, which is available in the framework through the getRequest() method call—this method returns an object of type org.restlet.data.Request.

Content negotiation and the HTTP Accept header

As per REST's architecture philosophy, a Restlet resource can provide multiple representations of the same resource. This is where the org.restlet.resource. Variant object in the represent() method comes into play.

Before providing multiple resource representations, we need to tell the resource what kind of representations we support. We provide the variants in the resource's constructor, as follows:

```
public class AResource extends Resource {
public AResource(Context context, Request request, Response response)
{
        super(context, request, response);

        getVariants().add(new Variant(MediaType.APPLICATION_XML));
        getVariants().add(new Variant(MediaType.APPLICATION_JSON));
    }

    @Override
    public boolean allowGet() {
        return true;
    }

    @Override
```

```
        public Representation represent(Variant variant) throws
        ResourceException {
            if (MediaType.APPLICATION_XML.equals(variant.getMediaType()))
    {

                return new StringRepresentation(new String("xml"),
                    MediaType.APPLICATION_XML);
            } else if
            (MediaType.APPLICATION_JSON.equals(variant.getMediaType())) {
                representation = new StringRepresentation(new
                    String("json"), MediaType.APPLICATION_JSON);
            }
            return null;
        }
    }
```

In this example, we only use XML and JSON representations, but we can provide a variety of MIME types (for full details, see the Restlet 1.1 API documentation). Second, we need to handle the HTTP GET requests according to the client's requested variant (that is, MIME type). The requested variant comes in the HTTP *Accept* header of the request, and Restlet automatically provides its value in the variant object. We, therefore, need to check what variant type is being requested so that we return the appropriate representation. This is accomplished in the `represent()` method with the `if/else` statements, as follows:

```
    if (MediaType.APPLICATION_XML.equals(variant.getMediaType())) {
        return new StringRepresentation(new String("xml"),
            MediaType.APPLICATION_XML);
    } else if (MediaType.APPLICATION_JSON.equals(variant.getMediaType()))
    {
        return new StringRepresentation(new String("json"),
            MediaType.APPLICATION_JSON);
    }
```

We compare the requested variant to a value the resource supports and send a representation accordingly.

 If the MIME type requested in the *Accept* header of a request has not been explicitly set in the constructor of the resource, Restlet will return an error message stating so.

HTTP POST

Similar to our GET request, we override two methods so that a resource handles POST requests. We override the `allowPost()` and `acceptRepresentation()` methods, as follows:

```
public class AResource extends Resource {
    @Override
    public boolean allowPost() {
        return true;
    }

    @Override
    public void acceptRepresentation(Representation entity) throws
    ResourceException {
        String xml = entity.getText();
    }
}
```

With a POST request we also get a payload. The payload is made available by Restlet in the `entity` object of type `org.restlet.resource.Representation`. We can do different things with this instance, but because in this example we assume the payload is an XML representation, we get the full text of the payload through `entity.getText()`.

The representation stored in the `entity` object doesn't have to be an XML structure. It could be, for example, an image or any type of binary stream. If we were accepting a binary stream, we would then need to use the appropriate representation type such as a `java.io.InputStream` and use the `entity.getStream()` method call.

HTTP PUT

To accept PUT requests, we override the `allowPut()` method together with the `storeReprsentation()` method, as follows:

```
public class AResource extends Resource {
    @Override
    public boolean allowPut() {
        return true;
    }

    @Override
    public void storeRepresentation(Representation entity) throws
    ResourceException {
        String xml = entity.getText();
    }
}
```

The PUT method behaves similarly to a POST request, and we access the payload of the request calling the method `entity.getText()`.

HTTP DELETE

Finally, for DELETE requests, we have the same overriding pattern: we override the `allowDetele()` and `removeRepresentation()` methods. In code, this looks as follows:

```
public class AResource extends Resource {
    @Override
    public boolean allowDelete() {
        return true;
    }

    @Override
    public void removeRepresentation(Representation entity) throws
    ResourceException {
        String username = (String) getRequest().getAttributes()
            .get("username");
    }
}
```

Because we are passing a variable in the URI when deleting resources, we use the same idea we used for GET requests. If we have a URI /users/{username} with an HTTP request of DELETE, we get access to the `username` variable via the `org.restlet.data.Request` instance of the resource class. In other words, the value of the variable is now referenced in the String object, `username`.

As we know, not all URIs need to support all the HTTP request method types (GET, POST, PUT, DELETE).

If any of the resources we implement in Restlet 1.1 don't support any of the HTTP request types, we just don't override the corresponding methods. Specifically, we don't need to override the `allowXXX()` methods to return `false`, as they are defaulted to ignore any requests. However, this also means that if we have overridden any of the methods to handle a request—`represent()`, `acceptRepresentation()`, `udpateRepresentation()`, `deleteRepresentation()`—but not the corresponding `allowXXX()` methods, our service will throw an error message stating that the method requested can't be handled by the resource.

Implementation using Restlet 1.1

As we discussed, a Restlet web service is composed of a Restlet application class and Restlet resource classes that ultimately handle HTTP requests. For our 1.1 implementation, we first look at the web application configuration and then move onto URI mappings and request handlers.

Restlet application and URI mappings

Before our web container passes HTTP requests to our Restlet web service, we need to configure the framework in the web.xml file of the Java web application, as follows:

```xml
<?xml version="1.0" encoding="UTF-8"?>
<web-app version="2.4"
    xmlns="http://java.sun.com/xml/ns/j2ee"
    xmlns:xsi="http://www.w3.org/2001/XMLSchema-instance"
    xsi:schemaLocation="http://java.sun.com/xml/ns/j2ee
    http://java.sun.com/xml/ns/j2ee/web-app_2_4.xsd">
 <!-- This is the Restlet application. -->
 <context-param>
    <param-name>org.restlet.application</param-name>
    <param-value>web.RESTfulJavaWebService</param-value>
 </context-param>
 <!-- This should always be here for Restlet. -->
 <servlet>
    <servlet-name>RESTfulJavaWebService</servlet-name>
    <servlet-class>
        com.noelios.restlet.ext.servlet.ServerServlet
    </servlet-class>
 </servlet>
 <servlet-mapping>
    <servlet-name>RESTfulJavaWebService</servlet-name>
    <url-pattern>/*</url-pattern>
 </servlet-mapping>
</web-app>
```

For any Restlet 1.1 deployment, you'll need the following libraries in your web application's WEB-INF/lib directory. For Restlet 1.1: om.noelios. restlet.ext.servlet_2.5.jar, com.noelios.restlet.jar, org.restlet.jar.

For Db4o (only if you're using it): db4o-7.4.88.12908-java5.jar.

With our web application now properly routing requests to a Restlet application class, we look at the web service implementation, beginning with our application class. The full listing for the application class looks as follows:

```
package web;

import org.restlet.Application;
import org.restlet.Context;
import org.restlet.Restlet;
import org.restlet.Router;

public class RESTfulJavaWebService extends Application {

    public RESTfulJavaWebService(Context parentContext) {
        super(parentContext);
    }

    @Override
    public synchronized Restlet createRoot() {
        Router router = new Router(getContext());

        // Define routers for users
        router.attach("/users", UsersResource.class);
        router.attach("/users/{username}", UserResource.class);;

        // Define routers for messages
        router.attach("/messages", MessagesResource.class);
        router.attach("/messages/{messageID}",
            MessageResource.class);
        router.attach("/messages/users/{username}",
            UserMessagesResource.class);

        // Searching URI
        router.attach("/messages/search/{search_item}",
            SearchMessagesResource.class);

        return router;
    }
}
```

The instance of our `org.restlet.Application` class has a runtime context within the web server — the context is available through the `getContext()` method call. This context can be mapped to an `org.restlet.Router` object in which to attach unique Restlet resources — the request handlers. Specifically, we map each URI to a resource class in the overridden `createRoot()` method. The `createRoot()` method returns a `org.restlet.Restlet` object and the framework takes care of the rest.

We attach resources with the following statements (we only show two here):

```
Router router = new Router(getContext());
router.attach("/users", UsersResource.class);
router.attach("/messages/{messageID}", MessageResource.class);
```

URIs and resources

With our URIs mapped to corresponding resources, we now move onto the code for the Restlet resource classes. We begin with the code for our URI /users.

/users

The full listing for the UsersResource class looks as follows:

```
package web;

import java.io.IOException;

import org.restlet.Context;
import org.restlet.data.MediaType;
import org.restlet.data.Request;
import org.restlet.data.Response;
import org.restlet.data.Status;
import org.restlet.resource.Representation;
import org.restlet.resource.Resource;
import org.restlet.resource.ResourceException;
import org.restlet.resource.StringRepresentation;
import org.restlet.resource.Variant;

import exception.InvalidXMLException;
import exception.ItemAlreadyExistsException;

import business.UserBO;

public class UsersResource extends Resource {
    public UsersResource(Context context, Request request, Response
    response) {
        super(context, request, response);

        getVariants().add(new Variant(MediaType.APPLICATION_XML));
        getVariants().add(new Variant(MediaType.APPLICATION_JSON));
    }

    @Override
    public boolean allowGet() {
        return true;
    }
```

```
    @Override
    public Representation represent(Variant variant) throws
    ResourceException {
        Representation representation = null;

        if (MediaType.APPLICATION_XML.equals(variant.getMediaType()))
        {
            representation = new
                StringRepresentation(UserBO.getAllXML(),
                    MediaType.APPLICATION_XML);
        } else if
        (MediaType.APPLICATION_JSON.equals(variant.getMediaType())) {
            representation = new
                StringRepresentation(UserBO.getAllJSON(),
                    MediaType.APPLICATION_JSON);
        }

        return representation;
    }

    @Override
    public boolean allowPost() {
        return true;
    }

    @Override
    public void acceptRepresentation(Representation entity) throws
    ResourceException {
        try {
            Representation representation = new
                StringRepresentation(UserBO.create(entity.getText()),
                    MediaType.APPLICATION_XML);
            getResponse().setEntity(representation);
        } catch (InvalidXMLException e) {
            getResponse().setStatus(Status.CLIENT_ERROR_BAD_REQUEST);
        } catch (ItemAlreadyExistsException e) {
            getResponse().setStatus(Status.CLIENT_ERROR_FORBIDDEN);
        } catch (IOException e) {
            getResponse().setStatus(Status.SERVER_ERROR_INTERNAL );
        }
    }
}
```

In the constructor, we specify the two MIME types that the resource provides. We set the variant types with the lines:

```
getVariants().add(new Variant(MediaType.APPLICATION_XML));
getVariants().add(new Variant(MediaType.APPLICATION_JSON));
```

HTTP GET

After the `allowGet()` method is overridden and coded to return a value of `true`, we handle a GET request with the method:

```
@Override
public Representation represent(Variant variant) throws
ResourceException {
    Representation representation = null;
    if (MediaType.APPLICATION_XML.equals(variant.getMediaType()))
    {
        representation = new
            StringRepresentation(UserBO.getAllXML(),
                MediaType.APPLICATION_XML);
} else if
(MediaType.APPLICATION_JSON.equals(variant.getMediaType())) {
    representation = new StringRepresentation(UserBO.getAllJSON(),
        MediaType.APPLICATION_JSON);
    }

    return representation;
}
```

For this resource, we have two variant types: XML and JSON. As explained already, content negotiation is executed in the `represent()` method: the calling client sets the HTTP *Accept* header to a MIME type it can consume, and Restlet automatically makes the value available as an `org.restlet.resource.Variant` object. We, then, compare the requested MIME type to a value that the resource knows how to serve. If we have a match, we return a representation as an instance of the `org.restlet.resource.StringRepresentation` object.

How do we get the required structure? We get it from the business layer, with the call to `UserBO.getAllXML()` for an XML representation, or the call to `UserBO.getAllJSON()` for a JSON representation.

HTTP POST

After the `allowPost()` method is overridden and coded to return a value of `true`, we handle a POST request with the method:

```
@Override
public void acceptRepresentation(Representation entity) throws
ResourceException {
    try {
        Representation representation = new
            StringRepresentation(UserBO.create(entity.getText()),
                MediaType.APPLICATION_XML);
        getResponse().setEntity(representation);
    } catch (InvalidXMLException e) {
        getResponse().setStatus(Status.CLIENT_ERROR_BAD_REQUEST);
    } catch (ItemAlreadyExistsException e) {
        getResponse().setStatus(Status.CLIENT_ERROR_FORBIDDEN);
    } catch (IOException e) {
        getResponse().setStatus(Status.SERVER_ERROR_INTERNAL );
    }
}
```

The XML representation of a new user is available to us in the `entity` object, through the `getText()` method call. We delegate the creation of the resource to our business layer, with the call to the `UserBO.create()` method. After we have validated the XML representation and created the new user resource, we return the stored representation back to the client. We do this by setting the representation into the response object, with the line:

```
getResponse().setEntity(representation);
```

Finally, if any errors are found while creating a user resource—if the XML representation is invalid or the user identifier already exists—we catch the thrown exceptions from the business layer and set an appropriate status in the framework's response stream. Setting a failure status into the response stream is done with the line similar to:

```
getResponse().setStatus(Status.CLIENT_ERROR_BAD_REQUEST);
```

/users/{username}

The full listing of the `UserResource` class looks as follows:

```
package web;

import java.io.IOException;

import org.restlet.Context;
import org.restlet.data.MediaType;
import org.restlet.data.Request;
import org.restlet.data.Response;
import org.restlet.data.Status;
import org.restlet.resource.Representation;
import org.restlet.resource.Resource;
import org.restlet.resource.ResourceException;
import org.restlet.resource.StringRepresentation;
import org.restlet.resource.Variant;

import exception.InvalidXMLException;
import exception.ItemNotFoundException;

import business.UserBO;

public class UserResource extends Resource {
    public UserResource(Context context, Request request, Response
response) {
        super(context, request, response);

        getVariants().add(new Variant(MediaType.APPLICATION_XML));
        getVariants().add(new Variant(MediaType.APPLICATION_JSON));
    }

    @Override
    public boolean allowGet() {
        return true;
    }

    @Override
    public Representation represent(Variant variant) throws
ResourceException {
        Representation representation = null;
        String username = (String) getRequest().getAttributes()
            .get("username");

        if (MediaType.APPLICATION_XML.equals(variant.getMediaType()))
        {
            representation = new
                StringRepresentation(UserBO.getXML(username),
                    MediaType.APPLICATION_XML);
```

```
        } else if
          (MediaType.APPLICATION_JSON.equals(variant.getMediaType()))
        {
            representation = new
                StringRepresentation(UserBO.getJSON(username),
                    MediaType.APPLICATION_JSON);
        }

        return representation;
    }

    @Override
    public boolean allowPut() {
        return true;
    }

    @Override
    public void storeRepresentation(Representation entity) throws
    ResourceException {
        try {
            Representation representation = new
                StringRepresentation(UserBO.update(entity.getText()),
                    MediaType.APPLICATION_XML);
            getResponse().setEntity(representation);
        } catch (InvalidXMLException e) {
            getResponse().setStatus(Status.CLIENT_ERROR_BAD_REQUEST);
        } catch (ItemNotFoundException e) {
            getResponse().setStatus(Status.CLIENT_ERROR_NOT_FOUND);
        } catch (IOException e) {
            getResponse().setStatus(Status.SERVER_ERROR_INTERNAL );
        }
    }

    @Override
    public boolean allowDelete() {
        return true;
    }

    @Override
    public void removeRepresentations() throws ResourceException {
        try {
            String username = (String) getRequest().getAttributes()
                .get("username");
            UserBO.delete(username);
            getResponse().setStatus(Status.SUCCESS_NO_CONTENT);
        } catch (ItemNotFoundException e) {
            getResponse().setStatus(Status.CLIENT_ERROR_NOT_FOUND);
        }
    }
}
```

HTTP GET

In the constructor, we add two resource types: XML and JSON. After we override the `allowGet()` method to return `true`, we handle GET requests with the method:

```
@Override
public Representation represent(Variant variant) throws
ResourceException {
    Representation representation = null;
    String username = (String) getRequest().getAttributes()
        .get("username");
    if (MediaType.APPLICATION_XML.equals(variant.getMediaType()))
    {
        representation = new
            StringRepresentation(UserBO.getXML(username),
                MediaType.APPLICATION_XML);
    } else if
        (MediaType.APPLICATION_JSON.equals(variant.getMediaType()))
        {
        representation = new
            StringRepresentation(UserBO.getJSON(username),
                MediaType.APPLICATION_JSON);
    }

    return representation;
}
```

The `username` variable is part of the URI, and we get its value from the `org.restlet.data.Request` instance as follows:

```
String username = (String) getRequest().getAttributes()
                                        .get("username");
```

With the variable now referenced, we pass it to our business layer with the call to either the `UserBO.getXML` method (for an XML representation) or the `UserBO.getJSON()` method (for a JSON representation). Finally, an XML or a JSON representation is returned in the response stream.

HTTP PUT

After overriding the `allowPut()` method to return `true`, we handle user resource updates with the method:

```
@Override
public void storeRepresentation(Representation entity) throws
ResourceException {
    try {
```

```
        Representation representation = new
            StringRepresentation(UserBO.update(entity.getText()),
                MediaType.APPLICATION_XML);
        getResponse().setEntity(representation);
    } catch (InvalidXMLException e) {
        getResponse().setStatus(Status.CLIENT_ERROR_BAD_REQUEST);
    } catch (ItemNotFoundException e) {
        getResponse().setStatus(Status.CLIENT_ERROR_NOT_FOUND);
    } catch (IOException e) {
        getResponse().setStatus(Status.SERVER_ERROR_INTERNAL );
    }
}
```

We pass the value of the request's payload to our business layer through the method call:

```
Representation representation = new
    StringRepresentation(UserBO.update(entity.getText()),
        MediaType.APPLICATION_XML);
```

We send back to the caller the updated resource representation in the response stream, with the statement:

```
getResponse().setEntity(representation);
```

Finally, if any exceptions are thrown, we catch them and modify the response's status to an appropriate error code.

HTTP DELETE

With the `allowDelete()` method overridden to return `true`, we handle resource delete requests with the method:

```
@Override
public void removeRepresentations() throws ResourceException {
    try {
        String username = (String) getRequest().getAttributes()
            .get("username");
        UserBO.delete(username);
        getResponse().setStatus(Status.SUCCESS_NO_CONTENT);
    } catch (ItemNotFoundException e) {
        getResponse().setStatus(Status.CLIENT_ERROR_NOT_FOUND);
    }
}
```

First, we grab the value of the runtime variable in the URI from the `org.restlet.data.Request` object. Then, we call our business layer helper method, `UserBO.delete()`. Finally, if exceptions are thrown by the business layer, we update the response stream with an appropriate error code.

/messages

The full listing of the `MessagesResource` class looks like:

```
package web;

import java.io.IOException;

import org.restlet.Context;
import org.restlet.data.MediaType;
import org.restlet.data.Request;
import org.restlet.data.Response;
import org.restlet.data.Status;
import org.restlet.resource.Representation;
import org.restlet.resource.Resource;
import org.restlet.resource.ResourceException;
import org.restlet.resource.StringRepresentation;
import org.restlet.resource.Variant;

import business.MessageBO;
import exception.InvalidXMLException;
import exception.UserNotFoundException;

public class MessagesResource extends Resource {
    public MessagesResource(Context context, Request request,
    Response response) {
        super(context, request, response);

        getVariants().add(new Variant(MediaType.APPLICATION_XML));
        getVariants().add(new Variant(MediaType.APPLICATION_JSON));
    }

    @Override
    public boolean allowGet() {
        return true;
    }


    @Override
    public Representation represent(Variant variant) throws
    ResourceException {
        Representation representation = null;

        if (MediaType.APPLICATION_XML.equals(variant.getMediaType()))
        {
            representation = new
                StringRepresentation(MessageBO.getAllXML(),
                    MediaType.APPLICATION_XML);
        } else if
          (MediaType.APPLICATION_JSON.equals(variant.getMediaType()))
            {
```

```
            representation = new
                StringRepresentation(MessageBO.getAllJSON(),
                    MediaType.APPLICATION_JSON);
        }

        return representation;
    }

    @Override
    public boolean allowPost() {
        return true;
    }

    @Override
    public void acceptRepresentation(Representation entity) throws
    ResourceException {
        try {
            Representation representation = new
              StringRepresentation(MessageBO.create(entity.getText()),
                  MediaType.APPLICATION_XML);
            getResponse().setEntity(representation);
        } catch (InvalidXMLException e) {
            getResponse().setStatus(Status.CLIENT_ERROR_BAD_REQUEST);
        } catch (UserNotFoundException e) {
            getResponse().setStatus(Status.CLIENT_ERROR_NOT_FOUND);
        } catch (IOException e) {
            getResponse().setStatus(Status.SERVER_ERROR_INTERNAL);
        }
    }
}
```

This Restlet resource has the same coding pattern we used for /users.
The only difference is that we make calls to our MessageBO helper class, instead
of our UserBO class.

/messages/{messageID}

The full listing of the MessageResource class looks like:

```
package web;

import org.restlet.Context;
import org.restlet.data.MediaType;
import org.restlet.data.Request;
import org.restlet.data.Response;
import org.restlet.data.Status;
import org.restlet.resource.Representation;
```

```java
import org.restlet.resource.Resource;
import org.restlet.resource.ResourceException;
import org.restlet.resource.StringRepresentation;
import org.restlet.resource.Variant;

import business.MessageBO;
import exception.ItemNotFoundException;

public class MessageResource extends Resource {
    public MessageResource(Context context, Request request, Response
    response) {
        super(context, request, response);

        getVariants().add(new Variant(MediaType.APPLICATION_XML));
        getVariants().add(new Variant(MediaType.APPLICATION_JSON));
    }

    @Override
    public boolean allowGet() {
        return true;
    }

    @Override
    public Representation represent(Variant variant) throws
    ResourceException {
        Representation representation = null;
        String messageID = (String) getRequest().getAttributes()
            .get("messageID");

        if (MediaType.APPLICATION_XML.equals(variant.getMediaType()))
        {
            representation = new
                StringRepresentation(MessageBO.getXML(messageID),
                    MediaType.APPLICATION_XML);
        } else if
          (MediaType.APPLICATION_JSON.equals(variant.getMediaType()))
          {
            representation = new
                StringRepresentation(MessageBO.getJSON(messageID),
                    MediaType.APPLICATION_JSON);
        }

        return representation;
    }

    @Override
    public boolean allowDelete() {
        return true;
    }
```

```
    @Override
    public void removeRepresentations() throws ResourceException {
        try {
            String messageID = (String) getRequest().getAttributes()
                .get("messageID");
            MessageBO.delete(messageID);
            getResponse().setStatus(Status.SUCCESS_NO_CONTENT);
        } catch (ItemNotFoundException e) {
            getResponse().setStatus(Status.CLIENT_ERROR_NOT_FOUND);
        }
    }
}
```

This Restlet resource has the same coding pattern used for /users/{username},
with the difference that we are now dealing with messages. Therefore, we make calls
to MessageBO, instead of UserBO. In addition, we don't allow message updates, as we
do for users.

/messages/users/{username}

The full listing of the UserMessagesResource class looks like:

```
package web;

import org.restlet.Context;
import org.restlet.data.MediaType;
import org.restlet.data.Request;
import org.restlet.data.Response;
import org.restlet.resource.Representation;
import org.restlet.resource.Resource;
import org.restlet.resource.ResourceException;
import org.restlet.resource.StringRepresentation;
import org.restlet.resource.Variant;

import business.MessageBO;

public class UserMessagesResource extends Resource {
    public UserMessagesResource(Context context, Request request,
    Response response) {
        super(context, request, response);

        getVariants().add(new Variant(MediaType.APPLICATION_XML));
        getVariants().add(new Variant(MediaType.APPLICATION_JSON));
    }

    @Override
    public boolean allowGet() {
        return true;
```

```
    }
    @Override
    public Representation represent(Variant variant) throws
    ResourceException {
        Representation representation = null;
        String username = (String) getRequest().getAttributes()
            .get("username");

        if (MediaType.APPLICATION_XML.equals(variant.getMediaType()))
        {
            representation = new
            StringRepresentation(MessageBO.getAllXMLForUser(username),
                MediaType.APPLICATION_XML);
        } else if
            (MediaType.APPLICATION_JSON.equals(variant.getMediaType()))
        {
            representation = new
            StringRepresentation(MessageBO.getAllJSONForUser(username),
                MediaType.APPLICATION_JSON);
        }

        return representation;
    }
}
```

For this resource we only provide a handler for HTTP GET requests. Further, more we provide two representation types: XML and JSON. The URI pattern passes in the value of a user's unique identifier; therefore, we need to, first, retrieve the identifier from the request object, and, second, once we have the value of this identifier, we pass it to our business layer to either the `MessageBO.getAllXMLForUser()` or the `MessageBO.getAllJSONForUser()` method. The returned structure of either of these methods is set as a Restlet representation in the response stream.

/messages/search/{search_item}

The full listing of the `SearchMessagesResource` class looks like:

```
package web;

import org.restlet.Context;
import org.restlet.data.MediaType;
import org.restlet.data.Request;
import org.restlet.data.Response;
import org.restlet.resource.Representation;
import org.restlet.resource.Resource;
import org.restlet.resource.ResourceException;
import org.restlet.resource.StringRepresentation;
```

```
import org.restlet.resource.Variant;

import business.MessageBO;

public class SearchMessagesResource extends Resource {
    public SearchMessagesResource(Context context, Request request,
    Response response) {
        super(context, request, response);

        getVariants().add(new Variant(MediaType.APPLICATION_XML));
        getVariants().add(new Variant(MediaType.APPLICATION_JSON));
    }

    @Override
    public boolean allowGet() {
        return true;
    }

    @Override
    public Representation represent(Variant variant) throws
    ResourceException {
        Representation representation = null;
        String search_item = (String) getRequest().getAttributes()
            .get("search_item");

        if (MediaType.APPLICATION_XML.equals(variant.getMediaType()))
        {
            representation = new
            StringRepresentation(MessageBO.searchAllXML(search_item),
                MediaType.APPLICATION_XML);
        } else if
        (MediaType.APPLICATION_JSON.equals(variant.getMediaType()))
        {
            representation = new
            StringRepresentation(MessageBO.searchAllJSON(search_item),
                MediaType.APPLICATION_JSON);
        }

        return representation;
    }
}
```

This resource is similar to the one we discussed just before this one
(UserMessagesResource), and it has the same coding pattern: we retrieve the
value of the URI parameter and pass it to our business layer for execution; then,
we return the XML or JSON structure as the representation of the response stream.
The business layer call is now made to the MessageBO.searchAllXML() or the
MessageBO.searchAllJSON() method, depending on the value of HTTP header
Accept sent by the client.

With the implementation of this URI, we're done with coding our API with
Restlet 1.1. And we now move to web service development with Restlet 2.0.

Restlet 2.0

Restlet version 2.0 has gone through a refactoring phase, though the latest version keeps the same architectural pattern of version 1.1—that of an application class routing HTTP request to resource classes. Specifically, an application class extends `org.restlet.Application`, and each Resource class extends `org.restlet.resource.ServerResource`. Moreover, version 2.0 adds Java annotations to handle HTTP requests. The Restlet framework, however, doesn't implement JAX-RS. Therefore, as of this writing, Restlet's annotations are not to be confused or compared with Jersey's annotations, as they don't work the same way.

To continue, we now need to look at how version 2.0 provides URI mappings and how HTTP requests are handled with `org.restlet.resource.ServerResource` classes. We begin our exploration with the Restlet application class.

Restlet application and URI mappings

In Chapter 4, we defined six URIs. The URI to access a list of all users is `http://localhost:8080/users`. We said earlier that an application class routes requests to appropriate resources. An arbitrary sample of code to route this URI to its appropriate handling resource looks as follows:

```
public class AWebService extends Application {
    public RESTfulJavaWebService(Context parentContext) {
        super(parentContext);
    }
    @Override
    public synchronized Restlet createInboundRoot() {
        Router router = new Router(getContext());

        // Define routers for users
        router.attach("/users", UsersResource.class);
        router.attach("/users/{usename}", UserResource.class);
    }
}
```

We first extend `org.restlet.Application` and we override the method, `createInboundRoot()` (note that for version 1.1, we override the `createRoot()` method). In this method, we create an `org.restlet.routing.Router` object that is used to map URIs with Restlet resources. In our snippet of code here we are telling the framework that the URI /users is to be handled by the `UsersResource.class` class, and /users/{username} by `UserResource.class`.

With our Restlet application ready to accept HTTP requests, we move onto the details of how each request is serviced by Restlet resources attached to an `org.restlet.routing.Router` object. For this, the framework provides method annotations.

Annotations

Version 2.0 uses annotated resource methods to handle HTTP requests. It provides annotations for the HTTP requests GET, POST, PUT, and DELETE. Once an HTTP request has been delegated to a resource, it's up to the annotated method to handle each request.

@Get and content negotiation (HTTP Accept header)

This annotation is used for HTTP GET requests. The annotation definition is case sensitive and, therefore, for a GET request it must be typed as `@Get`. This annotation takes a parameter that allows producing specific representation MIME types. For example, the annotation `@Get("xml")` produces a representation of `application/xml` MIME type, and the annotation `@Get("json")` produces a representation of `application/json` MIME type.

The Restlet framework automatically serves a representation type, depending on the value of the HTTP header *Accept*. This means that the client making a request has to set up the correct representation type it can consume. If the Accept header is not part of the HTTP request, then the request is handled by the first annotated method; subsequently, if the *Accept* header is invalid, Restlet will return an appropriate error message.

In code, using this annotation for an arbitrary resource looks as follows:

```
public class UsersResource extends ServerResource {
    @Get("xml")
    public Representation getXML() {
        String xml = ...;
        return new StringRepresentation(xml,
                                    MediaType.APPLICATION_XML);
    }
    @Get("json")
    public Representation getJSON() {
        String json = ...;
        return new StringRepresentation(json,
                                    MediaType.APPLICATION_JSON);
    }
}
```

This resource provides two representations: XML and JSON.
The content of the representation is the returned value `org.restlet.`
`representation.Representation`.

Restlet provides multiple representation types in the package `org.restlet.`
`representation`, so we choose the most appropriate type for the problem we are
solving. For the implementation of our web service, we use the `org.restlet.`
`representation.StringRepresentation` type, which allows us creating an XML
or a JSON structure right from its constructor.

For a request with a runtime variable in the URI, we need to access the value of the
parameter. Thus, we get the value of the parameter as follows:

```
public class UserResource extends ServerResource {
    @Get("xml")
    public Representation getXML() {
        String username = (String) getRequest().getAttributes()
            .get("username");
    return new StringRepresentation(username,
        MediaType.APPLICATION_XML);
}
```

In this snippet of code, the URI is of the form `/users/{username}` and the value of
`username` is part of the request, to which we have access using the line:

```
String username = (String) getRequest().getAttributes()
    .get("username");
```

 The name of these annotated methods is arbitrary,
but we should use names representative of the problem domain.

@Post

We use this annotation to create new resources. A sample use of this annotation
looks as follows:

```
public class UserResource extends ServerResource {
    @Post
    public Representation createUser(Representation entity) {
        String xml = entity.getText();
        return new StringRepresentation(xml,
            MediaType.APPLICATION_XML);
    }
}
```

Restlet gives us access to the payload of the request through the `entity` object, which is of type `org.restlet.representation.Representation`.

We could convert the representation to a `org.restlet.data.Form` object to get access to a set of name/value pairs if the request comes from an HTML form. For our example, however, we assume the payload is an XML representation; therefore, we get the full text and just return it back to the caller.

@Put

This annotation works the same way the `@Post` annotation does. A sample of this annotation looks as follows:

```
public class UserResource extends ServerResource {
    @Put
    public Representation updateUser(Representation entity) {
        String xml = entity.getText();
        return new StringRepresentation(xml,
                                        MediaType.APPLICATION_XML);
    }
}
```

The payload of the PUT request is available to us through the `entity` object.

@Delete

When we are deleting a resource, we typically pass in a unique identifier as part of the URI. For example, if we were deleting a user with the URI /users/{username}, we'd use this annotation as follows:

```
public class UserResource extends ServerResource {
    @Get("xml")
    public void deleteUser() {
        String username = (String)getRequest().getAttributes()
            .get("username");
    }
}
```

Because the variable `username` is being passed in the URI, we need to get its value from the request object. Normally, a delete request doesn't have to return a representation; therefore, we return `void` in the method's signature.

> If a URI has been properly routed to a valid resource and a request method is not implemented (meaning, annotated), then Restlet automatically generates a *method not implemented* error message.

Implementation using Restlet 2.0

Similar to Restlet v1.1, we map URIs to Restlet resource classes. However, because of the refactoring phase in version 2.0, we have subtle differences in the implementation of resources, which we explain here.

Similar, to our Restlet 1.1 implementation, we first need to configure our web application that is to be deployed in our Java web container. We configure the web application with the `web.xml` file, which looks as follows:

```xml
<?xml version="1.0" encoding="UTF-8"?>
<web-app id="WebApp_ID" version="2.4"
         xmlns="http://java.sun.com/xml/ns/j2ee"
         xmlns:xsi="http://www.w3.org/2001/XMLSchema-instance"
         xsi:schemaLocation="http://java.sun.com/xml/ns/j2ee
              http://java.sun.com/xml/ns/j2ee/web-app_2_4.xsd">
    <display-name>RESTful Java Web Services - Restlet</display-name>
    <!-- Application class name -->
    <context-param>
      <param-name>org.restlet.application</param-name>
      <param-value>
         web.RESTfulJavaWebService
      </param-value>
    </context-param>
    <!-- Restlet adapter -->
    <servlet>
      <servlet-name>RestletServlet</servlet-name>
      <servlet-class>
        org.restlet.ext.servlet.ServerServlet
      </servlet-class>
    </servlet>
    <!-- Catch all requests -->
    <servlet-mapping>
      <servlet-name>RestletServlet</servlet-name>
      <url-pattern>/*</url-pattern>
    </servlet-mapping>
</web-app>
```

For any Restlet 2.0 deployment, you'll need the following libraries in your web application's `WEB-INF/lib` directory. For Restlet 2.0: `om.restlet.ext.servlet.jar`, `org.restlet.jar`.

For Db4o (only if you're using it): `db4o-7.4.88.12908-java5.jar`.

Restlet application and URI mappings

A Restlet web service uses the `org.restlet.Application` class that serves as the interceptor of HTTP requests. Our application class looks as follows:

```java
package web;

import org.restlet.Application;
import org.restlet.Context;
import org.restlet.Restlet;
import org.restlet.routing.Router;

public class RESTfulJavaWebService extends Application {
    public RESTfulJavaWebService(Context parentContext) {
        super(parentContext);
    }

    @Override
    public synchronized Restlet createInboundRoot() {
        Router router = new Router(getContext());

        // Define routers for users
        router.attach("/users", UsersResource.class);
        router.attach("/users/{username}", UserResource.class);
        // Define routers for messages
        router.attach("/messages", MessagesResource.class);
        router.attach("/messages/{messageID}",
            MessageResource.class);
        router.attach("/messages/users/{username}",
            UserMessagesResource.class);
        // Searching URI
        router.attach("/messages/search/{search_item}",
            SearchMessagesResource.class);

        return router;
    }
}
```

All we're doing in this class is mapping URIs to Restlet resource classes.

URIs and resources

A Restlet resource class extends `org.restlet.resource.ServerResource`. We begin with the resource for `/users`.

/users

The full listing for the `UsersResource` class looks as follows:

```
package web;

import java.io.IOException;

import org.restlet.data.MediaType;
import org.restlet.data.Status;
import org.restlet.representation.Representation;
import org.restlet.representation.StringRepresentation;
import org.restlet.resource.Get;
import org.restlet.resource.Post;
import org.restlet.resource.ServerResource;

import business.UserBO;
import exception.InvalidXMLException;
import exception.ItemAlreadyExistsException;

public class UsersResource extends ServerResource {
    @Get("xml")
    public Representation getXML() {
        String xml = UserBO.getAllXML();
        Representation representation = new StringRepresentation(xml,
            MediaType.APPLICATION_XML);

        return representation;
    }

    @Get("json")
    public Representation getJSON() {
        String json = UserBO.getAllJSON();
        Representation representation = new
                StringRepresentation(json, MediaType.APPLICATION_JSON);
        return representation;
    }

    @Post
    public Representation createtUser(Representation entity) {
        Representation representation = null;

        try {
            representation = new
                StringRepresentation(UserBO.create(entity.getText()),
                    MediaType.APPLICATION_XML);
        } catch (InvalidXMLException e) {
            setStatus(Status.CLIENT_ERROR_BAD_REQUEST);
            representation = new StringRepresentation("Invalid XML.",
                MediaType.TEXT_PLAIN);
```

```
    } catch (ItemAlreadyExistsException e) {
      setStatus(Status.CLIENT_ERROR_FORBIDDEN);
      representation = new StringRepresentation("Item already
         exists.", MediaType.TEXT_PLAIN);
    } catch (IOException e) {
      setStatus(Status.SERVER_ERROR_INTERNAL );
    }

    return representation;
  }
}
```

HTTP GET

We provide XML and JSON representations.

XML representation

The request for an XML representation is handled by the method:

```
@Get("xml")
public Representation getXML() {
    String xml = UserBO.getAllXML();
    Representation representation = new StringRepresentation(xml,
        MediaType.APPLICATION_XML);
    return representation;
}
```

Getting all messages as an XML representation takes no more work than calling the helper method `UserBO.getAllXML()`, which is part of our business layer and the same call we use for the implementation in Restlet 1.1. The XML structure sent back from the business layer is a String object. For our representation we use an `org.restlet.represntation.StringRepresentation` class, which takes as parameters the XML string and a MIME type that is represented by the `MediaType.APPLICATION_XML` constant. (For more representation types, check the Restlet 2.0 API documentation.)

JSON representation

A JSON representation of all users is handled by this method:

```
@Get("json")
public Representation getJSON() {
    String json = UserBO.getAllJSON();
    Representation representation = new
        StringRepresentation(json, MediaType.APPLICATION_JSON);

    return representation;
}
```

This method is only different from the previous XML representation in two ways: first, we call `UserBO.getAllJSON()`; second, we use the MIME type `MediaType.APPLICATION_JSON` for the constructor of the `org.restlet.represntation.StringRepresentation` object.

HTTP POST

Creating a new user is handled with the method:

```
@Post
public Representation createtUser(Representation entity) {
    Representation representation = null;
    try {
      representation = new
            StringRepresentation(UserBO.create(entity.getText()),
                MediaType.APPLICATION_XML);
    } catch (InvalidXMLException e) {
        setStatus(Status.CLIENT_ERROR_BAD_REQUEST);
        representation = new StringRepresentation("Invalid XML.",
            MediaType.TEXT_PLAIN);
    } catch (ItemAlreadyExistsException e) {
        setStatus(Status.CLIENT_ERROR_FORBIDDEN);
        representation = new StringRepresentation("Item already
            exists.", MediaType.TEXT_PLAIN);
    } catch (IOException e) {
        setStatus(Status.SERVER_ERROR_INTERNAL );
    }

    return representation;

}
```

We already know how to get the payload of the HTTP POST request (using the `entity.getText()` call). With the representation instance on hand, we now delegate the work of creating the user to our business layer. Specifically, we call `UserBO.create()`. This method call validates the XML representation sent by the client, and makes sure the user identifier doesn't already exist. If any errors are found, the business layer throws either an `InvalidXMLException` exception or an `ItemAlreadyExistsException` exception. When this happens, we need to tell the framework that an error has occurred by calling the method `setStatus()` — this method takes a status parameter, which is a constant defined in the `org.restlet.data.Status` class (for full details on the status codes, see the Restlet 2.0 API documentation).

/users/{username}

The full listing for the `UserResource` class looks as follows:

```
package web;

import java.io.IOException;

import org.restlet.data.MediaType;
import org.restlet.data.Status;
import org.restlet.representation.Representation;
import org.restlet.representation.StringRepresentation;
import org.restlet.resource.Delete;
import org.restlet.resource.Get;
import org.restlet.resource.Put;
import org.restlet.resource.ServerResource;

import business.UserBO;
import exception.InvalidXMLException;
import exception.ItemNotFoundException;

public class UserResource extends ServerResource {
    @Get("xml")
    public Representation getXML() {
        String username = (String) getRequest().getAttributes()
            .get("username");
        StringRepresentation representation = null;

        String xml = UserBO.getXML(username);
        representation = new StringRepresentation(xml,
            MediaType.APPLICATION_XML);
        if (xml != null) {
          return representation;
        } else {
          setStatus(Status.CLIENT_ERROR_NOT_FOUND);
          return null;
        }
    }

    @Get("json")
    public Representation getJSON() {
        String username = (String) getRequest().getAttributes()
            .get("username");
        StringRepresentation representation = null;
        String json = UserBO.getJSON(username);
        representation = new StringRepresentation(json,
            MediaType.APPLICATION_JSON);
        if (json != null) {
          return representation;
```

```
        } else {
            setStatus(Status.CLIENT_ERROR_NOT_FOUND);
            return null;
        }
    }

    @Put
    public Representation updateUser(Representation entity) {
        Representation representation = null;
        try {
            representation = new
                StringRepresentation(UserBO.update(entity.getText()),
                    MediaType.APPLICATION_XML);
        } catch (InvalidXMLException e) {
            setStatus(Status.CLIENT_ERROR_BAD_REQUEST);
            representation = new StringRepresentation("Invalid XML.",
                MediaType.TEXT_PLAIN);
        } catch (ItemNotFoundException e) {
            setStatus(Status.CLIENT_ERROR_NOT_FOUND);
            representation = new StringRepresentation("Item not
                found.", MediaType.TEXT_PLAIN);
        } catch (IOException e) {
            setStatus(Status.SERVER_ERROR_INTERNAL );
        }

        return representation;
    }

    @Delete
    public void deleteUser() {
        String username = (String) getRequest().getAttributes()
            .get("username");
        try {
            UserBO.delete(username);
            setStatus(Status.SUCCESS_NO_CONTENT);
        } catch (ItemNotFoundException e) {
            setStatus(Status.CLIENT_ERROR_NOT_FOUND);
        }
    }
}
```

HTTP GET

We provide XML and JSON representations.

XML representation

The request for an XML representation is handled by this method:

```
@Get("xml")
public Representation getXML() {
    String username = (String) getRequest().getAttributes()
        .get("username");
    StringRepresentation representation = null;

    String xml = UserBO.getXML(username);
    representation = new StringRepresentation(xml,
        MediaType.APPLICATION_XML);
    if (xml != null) {
      return representation;
    } else {
        setStatus(Status.CLIENT_ERROR_NOT_FOUND);
        return null;
    }
}
```

This annotated method handles GET requests for a particular user. The identifier is part of the URI; therefore, we need to get the runtime value from the `Request` object with the statement:

```
String username = (String) getRequest().getAttributes()
    .get("username");
```

We now delegate retrieving the resource, with the identifier `useraname`, to our business layer. If a resource with the given identifier doesn't exist, we set the proper status message in the response stream. We set the appropriate error message with the following line (note the difference when compared to version 1.1):

```
setStatus(Status.CLIENT_ERROR_NOT_FOUND);
```

JSON representation

A JSON representation of a user is handled by this method:

```
@Get("json")
public Representation getJSON() {
    String username = (String) getRequest().getAttributes()
        .get("username");
    StringRepresentation representation = null;

    String json = UserBO.getJSON(username);
    representation = new StringRepresentation(json,
        MediaType.APPLICATION_JSON);
    if (json != null) {
```

```
        return representation;
    } else {
        setStatus(Status.CLIENT_ERROR_NOT_FOUND);
        return null;
    }
}
```

The only difference in this method from the one providing an XML
representation is that we use the call to the `UserBO.getJSON()` method instead
of the `UserBO.getXML()` method.

HTTP PUT

We update a user resource with the method:

```
@Put
public Representation updateUser(Representation entity) {
    Representation representation = null;
    try {
        representation = new
            StringRepresentation(UserBO.update(entity.getText()),
                MediaType.APPLICATION_XML);
    } catch (InvalidXMLException e) {
        setStatus(Status.CLIENT_ERROR_BAD_REQUEST);
        representation = new StringRepresentation("Invalid XML.",
            MediaType.TEXT_PLAIN);
    } catch (ItemNotFoundException e) {
        setStatus(Status.CLIENT_ERROR_NOT_FOUND);
        representation = new StringRepresentation("Item not
            found.", MediaType.TEXT_PLAIN);
    } catch (IOException e) {
        setStatus(Status.SERVER_ERROR_INTERNAL );
    }

    return representation;
}
```

As we have already discussed, the payload of a PUT request is available to us in
the `entity` object of type, `org.restlet.represntation.Representation`. We
make a call to our business layer to the `UserBO.update()` method, with the XML
representation sent by the client as the input parameter. Once the business layer has
validated the XML and updated the resource in our data storage layer, we return
the stored XML representation back to the client. If any exceptions are thrown by
the business layer, we catch them and update the response status so that the client
knows errors were encountered during processing.

HTTP DELETE

We delete a user with the following method:

```
@Delete
public void deleteUser() {
    String username = (String) getRequest().getAttributes()
        .get("username");
    try {
        UserBO.delete(username);
        setStatus(Status.SUCCESS_NO_CONTENT);
    } catch (ItemNotFoundException e) {
        setStatus(Status.CLIENT_ERROR_NOT_FOUND);
    }
}
```

Deleting a user with the identifier username is handled by our business layer helper
UserBO.delete(). If errors are found, we catch the exceptions and update the
response status.

/messages

The full listing for the MessagesResource class looks as follows:

```
package web;

import java.io.IOException;

import org.restlet.data.MediaType;
import org.restlet.data.Status;
import org.restlet.representation.Representation;
import org.restlet.representation.StringRepresentation;
import org.restlet.resource.Get;
import org.restlet.resource.Post;
import org.restlet.resource.ServerResource;

import business.MessageBO;
import exception.InvalidXMLException;
import exception.UserNotFoundException;

public class MessagesResource extends ServerResource {
    @Get("xml")
    public Representation getXML() {
        String xml = MessageBO.getAllXML();
        Representation representation = new StringRepresentation(xml,
            MediaType.APPLICATION_XML);

        return representation;
    }
```

```
@Get("json")
public Representation getJSON() {
    String json = MessageBO.getAllJSON();
    Representation representation = new
        StringRepresentation(json, MediaType.APPLICATION_JSON);

    return representation;
}

@Post
public Representation createtMessage(Representation entity) {
    Representation representation = null;

    try {
        representation = new
         StringRepresentation(MessageBO.create(entity.getText()),
            MediaType.APPLICATION_XML);
    } catch (InvalidXMLException e) {
        setStatus(Status.CLIENT_ERROR_BAD_REQUEST);
        representation = new StringRepresentation("Invalid XML.",
            MediaType.TEXT_PLAIN);
    } catch (UserNotFoundException e) {
        setStatus(Status.CLIENT_ERROR_NOT_FOUND);
    } catch (IOException e) {
        setStatus(Status.SERVER_ERROR_INTERNAL);
    }

    return representation;
}
}
```

The coding pattern for messages is the same as we used for users. We don't introduce any new code, except that we use our `BusinessBO` helper class in our business layer, instead of our `UserBO` helper class.

/messages/{messageID}

The full listing for the `MessageResource` class looks as follows:

```
package web;

import org.restlet.data.MediaType;
import org.restlet.data.Status;
import org.restlet.representation.Representation;
import org.restlet.representation.StringRepresentation;
import org.restlet.resource.Delete;
import org.restlet.resource.Get;
import org.restlet.resource.ServerResource;
```

```
import business.MessageBO;
import exception.ItemNotFoundException;
public class MessageResource extends ServerResource {
    @Get("xml")
    public Representation getXML() {
        String messageID = (String) getRequest().getAttributes()
            .get("messageID");
        StringRepresentation representation = null;
        String xml = MessageBO.getXML(messageID);
        representation = new StringRepresentation(xml,
            MediaType.APPLICATION_XML);
        if (xml != null) {
            return representation;
        } else {
            setStatus(Status.CLIENT_ERROR_NOT_FOUND);
            return null;
        }
    }

    @Get("json")
    public Representation getJSON() {
        String messageID = (String) getRequest().getAttributes()
            .get("messageID");
        StringRepresentation representation = null;
        String json = MessageBO.getJSON(messageID);
        representation = new StringRepresentation(json,
            MediaType.APPLICATION_JSON);
        if (json != null) {
            return representation;
        } else {
            setStatus(Status.CLIENT_ERROR_NOT_FOUND);
            return null;
        }
    }

    @Delete
    public void deleteMessage() {
        String messageID = (String) getRequest().getAttributes()
            .get("messageID");
        try {
          MessageBO.delete(messageID);
          setStatus(Status.SUCCESS_NO_CONTENT);
        } catch (ItemNotFoundException e) {
            setStatus(Status.CLIENT_ERROR_NOT_FOUND);
        }
    }
}
```

The coding pattern for single messages is the same for single users, except that the calls to our business layers are done to `MessageBO` instead of `UserBO`. Furthermore, we don't allow for messages to be updated; therefore, we don't have an annotated `@Put` method.

/messages/users/{username}

The full listing for the `UserMessagesResource` class looks as follows:

```
package web;

import org.restlet.data.MediaType;
import org.restlet.representation.Representation;
import org.restlet.representation.StringRepresentation;
import org.restlet.resource.Get;
import org.restlet.resource.ServerResource;

import business.MessageBO;

public class UserMessagesResource extends ServerResource {
    @Get("xml")
    public Representation getXML() {
        String username = (String) getRequest().getAttributes()
            .get("username");
        String xml = MessageBO.getAllXMLForUser(username);
        Representation representation = new StringRepresentation(xml,
            MediaType.APPLICATION_XML);

        return representation;
    }

    @Get("json")
    public Representation getJSON() {
        String username = (String) getRequest().getAttributes()
            .get("username");
        String json = MessageBO.getAllJSONForUser(username);
        Representation representation = new
            StringRepresentation(json, MediaType.APPLICATION_JSON);

        return representation;
    }
}
```

HTTP GET

This resource only handles GET requests, and serves either an XML or a JSON representation, with a call to either `MessageBO.getAllXMLForUser()` or `MessageBO.getAllJSONForUser()`.

/messages/search/{search_item}

The full listing for the `SearchMessagesResource` looks as follows:

```java
package web;

import org.restlet.data.MediaType;
import org.restlet.representation.Representation;
import org.restlet.representation.StringRepresentation;
import org.restlet.resource.Get;
import org.restlet.resource.ServerResource;

import business.MessageBO;

public class SearchMessagesResource extends ServerResource {
    @Get("xml")
    public Representation getXML() {
        String search_item = (String) getRequest().getAttributes()
            .get("search_item");
        String xml = MessageBO.searchAllXML(search_item);
        Representation representation = new StringRepresentation(xml,
            MediaType.APPLICATION_XML);

        return representation;
    }

    @Get("json")
    public Representation getJSON() {
        String search_item = (String) getRequest().getAttributes()
            .get("search_item");
        String json = MessageBO.searchAllJSON(search_item);
        Representation representation = new
            StringRepresentation(json, MediaType.APPLICATION_JSON);

        return representation;
    }
}
```

HTTP GET

For an XML representation, we search for messages containing the string
`search_item` with `MessageBO.searchAllXML()`, for a JSON representation, with
`MessageBO.searchAllJSON()`. The searching is delegated to our business layer.

Summary

In this chapter, we covered the latest two officially released versions of the Restlet
framework. We implemented the web service we outlined in Chapter 4, with Restlet
versions 1.1 and 2.0, and were able to reuse a large portion of the code we developed
in Chapter 5 so that we could concentrate our study only on the web layer, the web
layer being the code needed to develop a fully-RESTful web service with Restlet.

We now move onto our next Java RESTful framework — JBoss's RESTEasy.
We'll follow the same approach: we'll study how the framework provides
RESTful facilities, and then study in detail how to implement our, now common,
web service requirements.

7

RESTEasy: JAX-RS

In this chapter, we implement the web service requirements we outlined in Chapter 4, *RESTful Web Services Design*, with the RESTEasy framework. RESTEasy is not only a RESTful framework, but is also JBoss's umbrella project that provides other frameworks to build RESTful web services. As part of the REST facilities, RESTEasy fully implements the JAX-RS specification. Subsequently, we only look at how we use RESTEasy to implement RESTful web services. At the time of this writing, the released version is 1.1GA.

Getting the tools

If you have already downloaded and installed Java's JDK and the Tomcat web server, you only need to download the JBoss's RESTEasy framework. Nevertheless, the complete list of the software needed for this chapter is as follows:

Software	Web location
Java JDK	`http://java.sun.com/`
Apache Tomcat	`http://tomcat.apache.org/download-60.cgi`
Db4o	`http://developer.db4o.com/files/default.aspx`
RESTEasy Framework	`http://www.jboss.org/resteasy/`

Install the latest Java JDK along with the latest version of Tomcat, if you haven't done so. Download and install Db4o and RESTEasy. Remember the location of the installs, as we'll need the libraries to deploy with the web application.

RESTEasy — a JAX-RS implementation

RESTEasy is a full open source implementation of the JAX-RS specification. This framework works within any Java Servlet container, but because it's developed by JBoss, it offers extra features that are not part of the JAX-RS requirements. For example, RESTEasy offers out-of-the-box Atom support and also offers seamless integration with the EJB container portion of JBoss (none of these features are explored here).

Web service architecture

By now, you should be familiar with the coding pattern we are following throughout this book. Because we want to reuse a large portion of code already written, we have separate layers of abstraction. In this chapter, therefore, we only talk about the web layer and study in detail how to implement a full RESTful web service using RESTEasy (if you want full details of every layer's implementation, see Chapter 5, *Jersey: JAX-RS*).

The full architecture of our web service looks as follows:

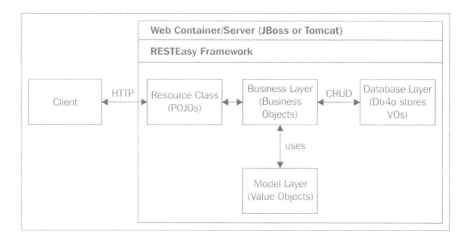

In this diagram, we depict clients making HTTP requests to our web service. Each request comes to the web container, which then delegates the request to our RESTful layer that is composed of RESTEasy resource classes. The actual serialization of user and message records is delegated to our business layer, which in turns talks directly to our database layer (a Db4o database).

Again, RESTEasy is a platform independent framework and works within any Servlet container. For this chapter we deploy our web service in Tomcat, as we've been working with it so far and are now familiar with deploying web applications to it, though we could as easily use the JBoss web container.

RESTful web service implementation with RESTEasy

In Chapter 4 we specified the API that we need to implement. We had six URIs that we now map to the following RESTEasy resource classes:

URI	Jersey resource class
`http://localhost:8080/users`	`UsersResource.class`
`http://localhost:8080/users/{username}`	`UserResource.class`
`http://localhost:8080/messages`	`MessagesResource.class`
`http://localhost:8080/messages/{messageID}`	`MessageResource.class`
`http://localhost:8080/messages/users/ {username}`	`UserMessagesResource. class`
`http://localhost:8080/messages/search/ {search_item}`	`SearchMessagesResource. class`

We implement the full API, and we list the full code for each resource.

To get the most out of this chapter, download the source code from `http://www.packtpub.com/files/code/6460_Code.zip` (look for `Chapter7`). With the source code downloaded, you can deploy the full application in your local machine and follow along with the code explanations.

Application deployment

The full listing of source code is as follows:

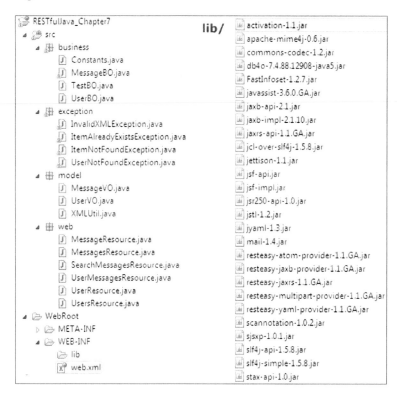

Before running the application, we need to tell the web server which Servlet handles HTTP requests. We do this by modifying the web.xml application descriptor as follows:

```xml
<?xml version="1.0"?>
<!DOCTYPE web-app PUBLIC "-//Sun Microsystems, Inc.//DTD Web
Application 2.3//EN"
        "http://java.sun.com/dtd/web-app_2_3.dtd">

<web-app>
    <display-name>RESTful Java Web Service</display-name>

    <!--  this tells RESTEasy to load resource classes -->
    <context-param>
        <param-name>resteasy.scan</param-name>
        <param-value>true</param-value>
    </context-param>

    <listener>
```

```
    <listener-class>
    org.jboss.resteasy.plugins.server.servlet.ResteasyBootstrap
    </listener-class>
</listener>

<servlet>
    <servlet-name>Resteasy</servlet-name>
    <servlet-class>
        org.jboss.resteasy.plugins.server.servlet
            .HttpServletDispatcher
    </servlet-class>
</servlet>

<servlet-mapping>
    <servlet-name>Resteasy</servlet-name>
    <url-pattern>/*</url-pattern>
</servlet-mapping>
</web-app>
```

This configuration file looks similar to the ones we have already seen in previous chapters. For RESTEasy, however, we need to specifically tell the framework to scan for resource classes within the web application context, because the default setting is to ignore resource classes. We do this with the following XML code:

```
<context-param>
    <param-name>resteasy.scan</param-name>
    <param-value>true</param-value>
</context-param>
```

Without this directive set to `true`, our application won't identify resource classes to handle HTTP requests.

Aside from this distinct web application configuration, a RESTEasy web service is deployable as a typical Java web application. Furthermore, for the framework to be available at runtime, we have to make sure all the libraries are available to the web application. The implementation libraries of the JAX-RS specification are available in the `/resteasy-jaxrs-1.1.GA/resteasy-jaxrs.war/WEB-INF/lib` directory (this is the location where you extracted the RESTEasy package). Remember to add all the JAR files in this directory to your web application's `WEB-INF/lib` directory as shown in the screenshot.

URI and resources

Because RESTEasy is a full implementation of the JAX-RS specification, we already have all the code for our web service. This also means that all the Java annotations that are already described in Chapter 5, *Jersey: JAX-RS*, apply to RESTEasy. Furthermore, all the details of the code have also been explained in Chapter 5. Nevertheless, we list all the code for the sake of completeness, as the RESTEasy implementation of the web service is a completely separate web application.

/users

With this URI we list all users and create users. The full listing of the UsersResource class looks as follows:

```
package web;

import javax.ws.rs.GET;
import javax.ws.rs.Path;
import javax.ws.rs.Produces;

import business.UserBO;

@Path("/users")
public class UsersResource {
    @GET
    @Produces("application/xml")
    public String getXML() {
        return UserBO.getAllXML();
    }

    @GET
    @Produces("application/json")
    public String getJSON() {
        return UserBO.getAllJSON();
    }

    @POST
    @Consumes("application/xml")
    @Produces("application/xml")
    public String createUser(String representation) {
        try {
            return UserBO.create(representation);
        } catch (InvalidXMLException e) {
            throw new WebApplicationException(400);
        } catch (ItemAlreadyExistsException e) {
            throw new WebApplicationException(403);
        }
    }
}
```

/users/{username}

With this URI we retrieve, update, and delete user records. The full listing for the UserResource class looks as follows:

```
package web;

import javax.ws.rs.Consumes;
import javax.ws.rs.DELETE;
import javax.ws.rs.GET;
import javax.ws.rs.PUT;
import javax.ws.rs.Path;
import javax.ws.rs.PathParam;
import javax.ws.rs.Produces;
import javax.ws.rs.WebApplicationException;

import business.UserBO;
import exception.InvalidXMLException;
import exception.ItemAlreadyExistsException;
import exception.ItemNotFoundException;

@Path("/users/{username}")
public class UserResource {
    @GET
    @Produces("application/xml")
    public String getXML(@PathParam("username") String username) {
        String xml = UserBO.getXML(username);
        if (xml != null) {
            return xml;
        } else {
            throw new WebApplicationException(404);
        }
    }

    @GET
    @Produces("application/json")
    public String getJSON(@PathParam("username") String username) {
        String json = UserBO.getJSON(username);
        if (json != null) {
            return json;
        } else {
            throw new WebApplicationException(404);
        }
    }

    @PUT
    @Consumes("application/xml")
    @Produces("application/xml")
    public String updateUser(@PathParam("username") username, String
            representation) {
        try {
```

```
            return UserBO.update(representation);
        } catch (InvalidXMLException e) {
        throw new WebApplicationException(400);
        } catch (ItemNotFoundException e) {
            throw new WebApplicationException(404);
        }
    }

    @DELETE
    public void deleteUser(@PathParam("username") String username) {
        try {
            UserBO.delete(username);
        } catch (ItemNotFoundException e) {
            throw new WebApplicationException(404);
        }
    }
}
```

/messages

With this URI we create messages and retrieve representations of messages.
The `MessagesResource` class looks as follows:

```
package web;

import javax.ws.rs.GET;
import javax.ws.rs.Path;
import javax.ws.rs.Produces;

import business.MessageBO;

@Path("/messages")
public class MessagesResource {
    @GET
    @Produces("application/xml")
    public String getXML() {
        return MessageBO.getAllXML();
    }

    @GET
    @Produces("application/json")
    public String getJSON() {
        return MessageBO.getAllJSON();
    }

    @POST
    @Consumes("application/xml")
    @Produces("application/xml")
    public String createMessage(String representation) {
```

```
                try {
                    return MessageBO.create(representation);
                } catch (InvalidXMLException e) {
                    throw new WebApplicationException(400);
                } catch (UserNotFoundException e) {
                    throw new WebApplicationException(403);
                }
            }
        }
```

/messages/{messageID}

With this URI we retrieve and delete messages. The full listing for the
MessageResource class looks as follows:

```
package web;

import javax.ws.rs.Consumes;
import javax.ws.rs.DELETE;
import javax.ws.rs.GET;
import javax.ws.rs.POST;
import javax.ws.rs.Path;
import javax.ws.rs.PathParam;
import javax.ws.rs.Produces;
import javax.ws.rs.WebApplicationException;

import business.MessageBO;
import exception.InvalidXMLException;
import exception.ItemNotFoundException;
import exception.UserNotFoundException;

@Path("/messages/{messageID}")
public class MessageResource {
    @GET
    @Produces("application/xml")
    public String getXML(@PathParam("messageID") String messageID) {
        String xml = MessageBO.getXML(messageID);
        if (xml != null) {
            return xml;
        } else {
            throw new WebApplicationException(404);
        }
    }

    @GET
    @Produces("application/json")
    public String getJSON(@PathParam("messageID") String messageID) {
```

```
        String json = MessageBO.getJSON(messageID);
        if (json != null) {
            return json;
        } else {
            throw new WebApplicationException(404);
        }
    }

    @DELETE
    public void deleteMessage(@PathParam("messageID")
        String messageID) {
      try {
          MessageBO.delete(messageID);
      } catch (ItemNotFoundException e) {
          throw new WebApplicationException(404);
      }
    }
}
```

/messages/users/{username}

With this URI we retrieve messages that have been added by a user with identifier username. The full listing for the UserMessagesResource class looks as follows:

```
package web;

import javax.ws.rs.GET;
import javax.ws.rs.Path;
import javax.ws.rs.PathParam;
import javax.ws.rs.Produces;

import business.MessageBO;

@Path("/messages/users/{username}")
public class UserMessagesResource {
    @GET
    @Produces("application/xml")
    public String getXML(@PathParam("username") String username) {
        return MessageBO.getAllXMLForUser(username);
    }

    @GET
    @Produces("application/json")
    public String getJSON(@PathParam("username") String username) {
        return MessageBO.getAllJSONForUser(username);
    }
}
```

/messages/search/{search_item}

With this URI we search messages that contain the term `search_item`. The full listing for the `SearchMessagesResource` class looks as follows:

```
package web;

import javax.ws.rs.GET;
import javax.ws.rs.Path;
import javax.ws.rs.PathParam;
import javax.ws.rs.Produces;

import business.MessageBO;

@Path("/messages/search/{search_item}")
public class SearchMessagesResource {
    @GET
    @Produces("application/xml")
    public String searchXML(@PathParam("search_item") String
            search_item) {
        return MessageBO.searchAllXML(search_item);
    }

    @GET
    @Produces("application/json")
    public String searchJSON(@PathParam("search_item") String
    search_item) {
        return MessageBO.searchAllJSON(search_item);
    }
}
```

Summary

In this chapter we have used RESTEasy's JAX-RS implementation to code our sample web service. Because it's a certified implementation of JAX-RS, we reused all the code we wrote in Chapter 5, including all the Java annotations specified in the JAX-311 specification. However, JBoss's RESTEasy open source umbrella project adds more functionality to fully integrate with JBoss technology stack, which is beyond the scope of this book. For more information on the RESTEasy project visit `http://www.jboss.org/resteasy/`.

Next, we'll cover our final RESTful framework, which is **Struts**.

8
Struts 2 and the REST Plugin

In this chapter, we use the Struts 2 framework (version 2.1.6) together with the REST plugin to implement the web service we defined in Chapter 4, *RESTful Web Services Design*.

It's not necessary for you to be familiar with Struts 2. However, it would help, as this chapter is not an introduction to the Struts 2 framework. Nevertheless, we cover enough of the framework to allow you to begin coding RESTful web services immediately. For example, we cover how to fully configure Struts 2 and the plugin, we explain how to map URIs to Struts 2 action classes, and we study in detail how each HTTP request is serviced by the plugin.

Getting the tools

For this chapter we need the latest version of Struts 2, which includes the REST plugin, together with the tools we already installed in previous chapters. The complete list of tools and their download locations are as follows:

Software	Web location
Java JDK	`http://java.sun.com/`
Apache Tomcat	`http://tomcat.apache.org/download-60.cgi`
Db4o	`http://developer.db4o.com/files/default.aspx`
Struts2 (2.1.6 or later)	`http://struts.apache.org/2.x/`

Install the latest Java JDK together with the latest version of Tomcat. Download and unpack Db4o and Struts 2, and remember the location of these packages, as we need to deploy a few JARs with our web application.

Struts 2

Struts 2 is a web development framework that is modelled after the **Model-View-Controller (MVC)** architectural pattern. It's built on top of the Java Servlet specification and works with any Java web server such as Tomcat or JBoss. The framework's intent is making web application development easier, because it provides automatic form validation, Java objects domain population, and internationalization of view renderings using JSP and custom tags.

The core of a Struts 2 application is the action class. In Struts 2 action classes are nothing more than **Plain Old Java Objects (POJOs)** that are bound to the framework through XML configuration and interface implementation. Any model object can become an action class, thus integrating model and view logic easily using action classes.

The framework is extendable through plugins that are added to any web application using JAR libraries. The REST plugin is one of these libraries and is now bundled with the standard Struts 2 package.

REST plugin

The REST plugin is a Struts 2 extension that adds REST support for the creation of web services. It implements the Ruby on Rails style of REST conventions, which is mainly a browser-centric implementation. For instance, the plugin supports automatic content negotiation through URIs and not through HTTP headers. The plugin also overloads the GET and POST request methods — using hidden form fields — to support resource updates, deletion, and creation because true PUT and DELETE HTTP requests are not supported by web browsers.

These compromises pose a small challenge when creating RESTful web services that are meant to be used with a variety of clients (web browsers, hand-held devices, and other web services). In other words, because of the current architecture of the plugin, we need to work around its limitations instead of implementing web services that have a standard architecture and follow the actual REST conventions.

 Our goal is to implement a fully compliant RESTful web service; therefore, we handle content negotiation through the HTTP *Accept* header and not through the URI. Furthermore, we support the true PUT and DELETE HTTP requests and we don't use hidden form fields in HTML forms to determine what needs to be done to a resource.

URI mappings

Whenever we encounter a new REST framework, we first need to identify how URI mapping is performed, and then we need to understand how each of the HTTP requests is handled within the framework.

The Struts 2 REST plugin depends on Struts 2 action class naming conventions for URI mapping, and strict adherence to predefined method names for request handling. The plugin looks for these specifically-named methods through reflection: if they are part of the class then they are used to handle the requests.

REST controller classes are the same as Struts 2 action classes; however, the naming convention makes differentiation between them easier (a REST action is a REST controller). These REST controller classes can live anywhere within the context of a web application, and their location is configurable using the `struts.xml` file.

A functional `struts.xml` file looks as follows:

```
<!DOCTYPE struts PUBLIC
    "-//Apache Software Foundation//DTD Struts Configuration 2.0//EN"
    "http://struts.apache.org/dtds/struts-2.0.dtd">

<struts>
    <constant name="struts.convention.action.suffix"
            value="Controller"/>
    <constant name="struts.convention.action.mapAllMatches"
            value="true"/>
    <constant name="struts.convention.default.parent.package"
            value="rest-default"/>
    <constant name="struts.convention.package.locators" value="web"/>
</struts>
```

The element `struts.convention.action.suffix` tells the framework that REST controller classes have the suffix `Controller`, so any class with this naming convention handles web service requests for the given URI that matches the class name. What does it mean for URIs to match controller names? Take for example the definition of our web service in Chapter 4, which requires that we implement the URIs `/users` and `/messages`. For the URI mapping to take effect within Struts 2 we need to code two different REST controllers: `UsersController` and `MessagesController` (the names before the suffix `Controller` *must* match the URIs).

Finally, with `struts.convention.package.locators`, we're telling the framework to look for REST controller classes in the *web* package. This package name is arbitrary and could be, for example, a name that represents your organization and project such as `com.yourcompany.yourwebservice.web`.

HTTP request handlers

The GET, POST, PUT, and DELETE HTTP requests are handled by specifically-named methods. Using the `/users` URI as an example, the method names for each request are mapped in the plugin as follows (method names are the same regardless of the controller's name):

HTTP Request	REST plugin method
GET - /users	index()
GET with a variable name - /users/{username}	show()
POST - /users	create()
PUT - /users/{username}	update()
DELETE - /users/{username}	destroy()

We now have enough information to code an action class that maps to our required URI /users (again, /users matches the *Users* part of `UsersController`):

```
public class UsersController {
    // GET /users
    public String index() {
        return "SUCCESS";
    }
    // GET /users/{username}
    public String show() {
        return "SUCCESS";
    }
    // POST /users
    public String create() {
        return "SUCCESS";
    }
    // PUT /users/{username}
    public String update() {
        return "SUCCESS";
    }
    // DELETE /users/{username}
    public String destroy() {
        return "SUCCESS";
    }
}
```

This snippet of code is a valid REST plugin controller, albeit a boring one. The return statement in each of the methods is telling the framework that actions have been completed successfully and that the controller is now passing the result to the view layer (this is standard Struts 2 functionality). Note that when a controller doesn't need to handle an HTTP request type we just leave its corresponding method out of the class.

Web service architecture

Our web service, as defined in Chapter 4, *RESTful Web Services*, maintains the same architecture we've used in the frameworks studied in previous chapters. Namely, we have a web layer that handles HTTP requests and a business layer that handles storing resources (the *model*) into a Db4o persistence layer. Because of this code layering, in this section, we only study how to implement the web layer using Struts 2 and the REST plugin. However, full details of the business and persistence layers can be found in Chapter 5, *Jersey: JAX-RS*.

The full architecture for our Struts 2 solution looks as follows:

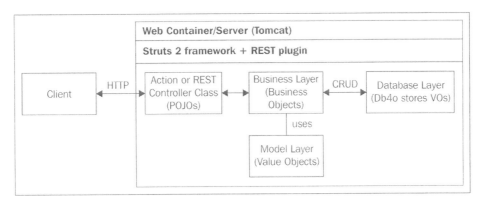

As depicted in this diagram, clients make HTTP requests to our web service using URIs. The requests are intercepted by Struts 2 and handled by the REST plugin in the form of REST controller classes. Resource serialization is handled by our business layer using a Db4o database.

RESTful web service implementation with Struts 2

In this section we use Struts 2 and the REST plugin to implement the six URIs required by our API. The mapping of URIs to REST controller classes is as follows:

URI	Jersey resource class
`http://localhost:8080/users`	`UsersController.class`
`http://localhost:8080/users/{username}`	
`http://localhost:8080/messages`	`MessagesController.class`
`http://localhost:8080/messages/{messageID}`	
`http://localhost:8080/usermessages/{username}`	`UsermessagesController.class`
`http://localhost:8080/searchmessages/{search_item}`	`SearchmessagesController.class`

Note that the last two URIs have changed from our original specification. This is a deliberate modification, because hierarchical URI mappings are not possible with the version of the plugin we're using. Our original specification requires that the last two URIs be of the form `/messages/users/{username}` and `/messages/search/{search_item}`. But because we can't technically comply with this requirement, we modify the API.

To get the most out of this section, download the source code from `http://www.packtpub.com/files/code/6460_Code.zip` (look for `Chapter8`) and follow along with the code explanations.

Application deployment

This is a traditional Java web application, with the following code tree:

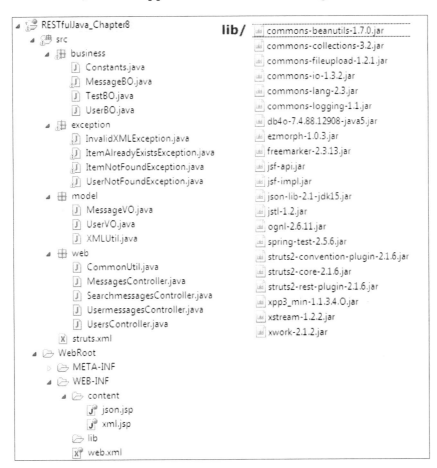

If you download the code, you can use the *lib* directory of the web application as your guide for what JAR files to include in your web services. However, all the libraries are also available in the software packages listed at the beginning of this chapter.

Because this is a Struts 2 web application, we need to configure the deployment using XML directives. The web application's `web.xml` configuration file looks as follows:

```
<?xml version="1.0" encoding="UTF-8"?>

<web-app id="starter" version="2.4"
        xmlns="http://java.sun.com/xml/ns/j2ee"
        xmlns:xsi="http://www.w3.org/2001/XMLSchema-instance"
        xsi:schemaLocation="http://java.sun.com/xml/ns/j2ee
                    http://java.sun.com/xml/ns/j2ee/web-app_2_4.xsd">
    <display-name>RESTful Java Web Services - Struts 2</display-name>
    <filter>
        <filter-name>RESTfulService</filter-name>
        <filter-class>
            org.apache.struts2.dispatcher.ng.filter
                .StrutsPrepareAndExecuteFilter
        </filter-class>
    </filter>
    <filter-mapping>
        <filter-name>RESTfulService</filter-name>
        <url-pattern>/*</url-pattern>
    </filter-mapping>
    <!-- Welcome file lists -->
    <welcome-file-list>
        <welcome-file>index.jsp</welcome-file>
    </welcome-file-list>
</web-app>
```

Everything in this file should be familiar to us: we let the web application direct requests to the Struts 2 framework within the context of the containing web application.

Because our web service uses the REST plugin, we also need to modify the `struts.xml` file as follows:

```
<?xml version="1.0" encoding="UTF-8" ?>

<!DOCTYPE struts PUBLIC
    "-//Apache Software Foundation//DTD Struts Configuration 2.0//EN"
    "http://struts.apache.org/dtds/struts-2.0.dtd">

<struts>
    <constant name="struts.convention.action.suffix"
                value="Controller"/>
```

```
            <constant name="struts.convention.action.mapAllMatches"
                   value="true"/>
            <constant name="struts.convention.default.parent.package"
                   value="rest-default"/>
            <constant name="struts.convention.package.locators"
                   value="web"/>
    </struts>
```

This is the same `struts.xml` file we looked at previously. Again, we tell the framework that we are using the REST plugin; then, we tell the framework to look for action classes that end with the suffix `Controller`; and we also tell the framework to look for REST controller classes in the *web* package. Finally, this file is located under the root of the source code, so that once deployed it's found in the root of the `classes` directory of the web application (see the `src` directory in the code tree listing).

URIs and resources

As we have already discussed, REST controllers are action classes that handle requests for specific URIs. We begin our study with the `UsersController` class, which handles the URIs `/users` and `/users/{username}`.

/users and /users/{username}

The full listing for the `UsersController` class looks as follows:

```
package web;

import java.io.IOException;
import javax.servlet.http.HttpServletRequest;
import org.apache.struts2.convention.annotation.Result;
import org.apache.struts2.convention.annotation.Results;
import org.apache.struts2.interceptor.ServletRequestAware;
import org.apache.struts2.rest.DefaultHttpHeaders;
import org.apache.struts2.rest.HttpHeaders;
import business.UserBO;
import com.opensymphony.xwork2.ModelDriven;
import exception.InvalidXMLException;
import exception.ItemAlreadyExistsException;
import exception.ItemNotFoundException;

@Results( { @Result(name = "success", type = "redirectAction") })
public class UsersController implements ModelDriven<Object>,
    ServletRequestAware {
    private String username;
    private String representation;
```

```
        private HttpServletRequest request;
        // GET /users
        public HttpHeaders index() {
            String acceptHeader = request.getHeader("Accept");
            String type = "xml";
            if (acceptHeader == null || acceptHeader.isEmpty()
                || acceptHeader.equals("application/xml")) {
                representation = UserBO.getAllXML();
            } else if (acceptHeader.equals("application/json")) {
                representation = UserBO.getAllJSON();
                type = "json";
            }

            return new DefaultHttpHeaders(type).disableCaching();
        }

        // GET /users/{username}
        public HttpHeaders show() {
            String acceptHeader = request.getHeader("Accept");
            String type = "xml";
            if (acceptHeader == null || acceptHeader.isEmpty() ||
                acceptHeader.equals("application/xml")) {
                 representation = UserBO.getXML(username);
            } else if (acceptHeader.equals("application/json")) {
                representation = UserBO.getJSON(username);
                type = "json";
            }

            return new DefaultHttpHeaders(type).disableCaching();
        }

        // POST /users
        public HttpHeaders create() {
            try {
                representation = UserBO.create(CommonUtil
                    .convertInputStreamToString(request
                        .getInputStream()));
            } catch (InvalidXMLException e) {
                throw new RuntimeException("Invalid XML.");
            } catch (ItemAlreadyExistsException e) {
                throw new RuntimeException("Item Exists.");
            } catch (IOException e) {
                throw new RuntimeException("Error reading input
                                            stream.");
            }

        return new DefaultHttpHeaders("xml").disableCaching();
```

```
    }
    // PUT /users/{username}
    public HttpHeaders update() {
        try {
            representation = UserBO.update(CommonUtil
                .convertInputStreamToString(request
                    .getInputStream()));
        } catch (InvalidXMLException e) {
            throw new RuntimeException("Invalid XML.");
        } catch (ItemNotFoundException e) {
            throw new RuntimeException("Username not found.");
        } catch (IOException e) {
            throw new RuntimeException("Error reading input
                                       stream.");
        }

        return new DefaultHttpHeaders("xml").disableCaching();
    }
    // DELETE /users/{username}
    public HttpHeaders destroy() {
        try {
            UserBO.delete(username);
        } catch (ItemNotFoundException e) {
            throw new RuntimeException("Username not found.");
        }

        return null;
    }
    public String getRepresentation() {
        return representation;
    }
    public Object getModel() {
        return representation;
    }
    public void setId(String id) {
        this.username = id;
    }
    public void setServletRequest(HttpServletRequest request) {
        this.request = request;
    }
}
```

A Struts 2 action class does three things: first, it accepts HTTP requests; second, it performs business logic with some data; and, third, it returns a result by redirecting logic to the appropriate view.

Now, let's dissect each method handling HTTP requests. We begin with the index() method, which handles GET requests.

HTTP GET /users

The method handling HTTP GET requests for a list of users is the index() method, as follows:

```
public HttpHeaders index() {
    String acceptHeader = request.getHeader("Accept");
    String type = "xml";
    if (acceptHeader == null || acceptHeader.isEmpty()
        || acceptHeader.equals("application/xml")) {
        representation = UserBO.getAllXML();
    } else if (acceptHeader.equals("application/json")) {
        representation = UserBO.getAllJSON();
        type = "json";
    }
    return new DefaultHttpHeaders(type).disableCaching();
}
```

In our web service specification we committed to provide XML and JSON resource representations; therefore, we need a way to automatically negotiate requested MIME types that doesn't use the default REST plugin solution, but uses the HTTP protocol together with the *Accept* header.

Out of the box, the REST plugin provides automatic content negotiation using URIs. For example, without doing any extra work, the framework converts the model, returned by the getModel() method, to XML with the URI /users.xml or to JSON with the URI /users.json. Even though this is a valid URI, it's not a RESTful request because we don't use the protocol to negotiate resource representations. In addition, because our business layer already has a mechanism to convert resources to either XML or JSON structures, we can't use the plugin functionality.

Automatic representation conversion through the URI is available only when the controller class implements the ModelDriven interface. Moreover, the conversion only happens for the object defined as the model in the getModel() method. For instance, if the model of an action class references a value object following the JavaBeans convention (proper getter and setter methods for its private members), then the plugin automatically converts the object's instance into an XML or JSON structure depending on the URI request (either ending with .xml or .json).

More important, however, we want to create a true RESTful web service, a service that properly handles the *Accept* header for content negotiation. We can do this in two ways: we could code a Struts 2 interceptor or we could manually grab the value of the header in the method where we need it.

For the sake of brevity, we opt for the latter option. First, we need access to the `javax.servlet.http.HttpServletRequest` instance of the HTTP request. Struts 2 action classes don't make this interface available, unless specifically told to do so. Thus, we implement the `org.apache.struts2.interceptor.ServletRequestAware` interface together with the `setServletRequest()` method, as follows:

```
public void setServletRequest(HttpServletRequest request) {
    this.request = request;
}
```

We define the `request` variable as a private member of the action class—the type of this variable is `javax.servlet.http.HttpServletRequest`.

We now have access to the value of the *Accept* header with the following statement:

```
String acceptHeader = request.getHeader("Accept");
```

Subsequently, we handle content negotiation with the following conditional statements:

```
if (acceptHeader == null || acceptHeader.isEmpty()
    || acceptHeader.equals("application/xml")) {
    representation = UserBO.getAllXML();
} else if (acceptHeader.equals("application/json")) {
    representation = UserBO.getAllJSON();
    type = "json";
}
```

This code states that if the *Accept* header is not set by the client or has the value of `application/xml`, we serve an XML representation of the resource by calling `UserBO.getAllXML()`. On the other hand, if the value of the header is `application/json`, we respectively call `UserBO.getAllJSON()`. Furthermore, we set the structure returned by the business layer as the model of the class. With a valid representation stored in the model (the model being the String object `representation`), we let the framework decide where to go next. In our case, the `HttpHeaders` return type tells the framework what view to display with the following return statement:

```
return new DefaultHttpHeaders(type).disableCaching();
```

How does the controller know to which view to delegate the work? It's a combination of the annotation at the beginning of the class and two JSP files. First, let's explain the annotation found at the beginning of each controller:

```
@Results( { @Result(name = "success", type = "redirectAction") })
```

This annotation tells the framework that the result mapped to `success` will be a redirect action and that whenever a redirect action is returned the framework needs to look for the view that is called either `xml.jsp` or `json.jsp`. This is the purpose of the `type` String object in the method: if the value of the header *Accept* is `null` or `application/xml` then we set `type = "xml"`; if the value is `application/json` then we set `type = "json"`.

Now let's explain what the `xml.sjp` and `json.jsp` files do. These are one-line JSP files that display the model according to the MIME type requested. The complete listing for the `json.jsp` file looks as follows:

```
<%@ page contentType="application/json; charset=UTF-8"%>
${representation}
```

And the complete listing for the `xml.jsp` file looks as follows:

```
<%@ page contentType="application/xml; charset=UTF-8"%>
${representation}
```

In both cases, we set the appropriate MIME type and let Struts 2 output the model's instance with the directive `${representation}`.

> What if the value of the *Accept* header is not `application/xml` or `application/json`? You can choose to return an error (handled by the framework), or add an `else` statement to handle all other cases and set the `type` object to XML. This way, a client will always receive something.

HTTP GET /users/{username}

The `show()` method handles GET requests for a user with identifier `username`, as follows:

```
public HttpHeaders show() {
    String acceptHeader = request.getHeader("Accept");
    String type = "xml";
    if (acceptHeader == null || acceptHeader.isEmpty() ||
        acceptHeader.equals("application/xml")) {
        representation = UserBO.getXML(username);
    } else if (acceptHeader.equals("application/json")) {
        representation = UserBO.getJSON(username);
```

```
            type = "json";
        }
        return new DefaultHttpHeaders(type).disableCaching();
    }
```

The logic for handling representation negotiation is the same as we explained earlier. However, we have a subtle difference, as we now have to account for the `username` variable in the URI. The REST plugin automatically makes the variable's value available using the `username` member in the action class. Once populated in the action's instance, we pass it as a parameter to the `UserBO.getXML()` or `UserBO.getJSON()` method.

> The `username` variable is automatically populated by the framework, as it uses the mapped variable `struts.mapper.idParameterName`. The name of this *id* variable is arbitrary, because the framework uses the setter method in the action class to populate it at runtime. For our class, the method we overwrite is `setId()`.

HTTP POST /users

The POST request to the `/users` URI creates new users, and is handled by the `create()` method, as follows:

```
public HttpHeaders create() {
    try {
        representation = UserBO.create(CommonUtil
            .convertInputStreamToString(request.getInputStream()));
    } catch (InvalidXMLException e) {
        throw new RuntimeException("Invalid XML.");
    } catch (ItemAlreadyExistsException e) {
        throw new RuntimeException("Item Exists.");
    } catch (IOException e) {
        throw new RuntimeException("Error reading input
                                    stream.");
    }
    return new DefaultHttpHeaders("xml").disableCaching();
}
```

The REST plugin was primarily designed to be used with web browsers. Consequently, HTML form processing for POST requests is standard. However, throughout this book, we talk about resources as representations that can be XML and JSON structures and not HTML form objects. What's more, our API requires that the payloads for POST and PUT requests are an XML representation of a given resource (it doesn't have to be, but we decided it to be so). This means that we can't use the default Struts 2 form processing to access the payload of POST and PUT requests. We, therefore, need to get access to the payload differently. Namely, we read the input stream of the request and convert it to a String object so that we can delegate the work to our business layer and create the respective resource.

Because we already made our controller request aware by implementing the `org.apache.struts2.interceptor.ServletRequestAware` interface, we get access to the `javax.servlet.http.HttpServletRequest` instance of every HTTP request. Therefore, we now have access to the payload of POST and PUT requests. More important, we can now convert it to something manageable such as a String object with the line:

```
representation = UserBO.create(CommonUtil
    .convertInputStreamToString(request.getInputStream()));
```

By definition, our API also returns back to the client the XML structure we verify and create with our business layer call to `UserBO.create()`. Therefore, we send back the representation to the client by setting the business layer result to the `representation` member. (Note that the `CommonUtil.convertInputStreamToString()` method is part of the source code for this chapter.)

HTTP PUT /users/{username}

The PUT request to a URI for a specific user, which updates a user's resource, is handled by the `update()` method, as follows:

```
public HttpHeaders update() {
    try {
        representation = UserBO.update(CommonUtil
            .convertInputStreamToString(request.getInputStream()));
    } catch (InvalidXMLException e) {
        throw new RuntimeException("Invalid XML.");
    } catch (ItemNotFoundException e) {
        throw new RuntimeException("Username not found.");
    } catch (IOException e) {
        throw new RuntimeException("Error reading input stream.");
    }

    return new DefaultHttpHeaders("xml").disableCaching();
}
```

Chapter 8

This request is similar to the POST request explained in the previous section. We have a payload that we need access to, though we make a different business call: we use `UserBO.update()` instead of `UserBO.create()`.

> For both request types, POST and PUT, the business layer throws different exceptions depending on the error encountered. For example, we can't create a user that already exists and we can't update a user that doesn't exist—both of these scenarios throw different exceptions for whatever the case may be.
>
> For the error handling in our implementation we throw the exceptions back to the user. However, with more time and space, we could be more forgiving and we could properly return HTTP-based error codes or XML-based error messages for easier client consumption. This is left as a coding exercise.

HTTP DELETE /users/{username}

The DELETE request deletes resource for a user with an identifier of `username`. The request is handled by the `destroy()` method, as follows:

```
public HttpHeaders destroy() {
    try {
        UserBO.delete(username);
    } catch (ItemNotFoundException e) {
        throw new RuntimeException("Username not found.");
    }
    return null;
}
```

Once again, we delegate the work to our business layer with the call to the method `UserBO.delete()`, for which we pass in the value of the variable in the URI (the `username` object).

/messages and /messages/{messageID}

The full listing for the `MessagesController` class looks as follows:

```
package web;

import java.io.IOException;
import javax.servlet.http.HttpServletRequest;
import org.apache.struts2.convention.annotation.Result;
import org.apache.struts2.convention.annotation.Results;
import org.apache.struts2.interceptor.ServletRequestAware;
import org.apache.struts2.rest.DefaultHttpHeaders;
```

[197]

```java
import org.apache.struts2.rest.HttpHeaders;
import business.MessageBO;
import com.opensymphony.xwork2.ModelDriven;
import exception.InvalidXMLException;
import exception.ItemNotFoundException;
import exception.UserNotFoundException;

@Results( { @Result(name = "success",
                    type = "redirectAction") })
public class MessagesController implements ModelDriven<Object>,
    ServletRequestAware {
    private String messageID;
    private String representation;
    private HttpServletRequest request;

    // GET /messages
    public HttpHeaders index() {

        String acceptHeader = request.getHeader("Accept");
        String type = "xml";
        if (acceptHeader == null || acceptHeader.isEmpty() ||
            acceptHeader.equals("application/xml")) {
            representation = MessageBO.getAllXML();
        } else if (acceptHeader.equals("application/json")) {
            representation = MessageBO.getAllJSON();
            type = "json";
        }

        return new DefaultHttpHeaders(type).disableCaching();
    }

    // GET /messages/{messageID}
    public HttpHeaders show() {
        String acceptHeader = request.getHeader("Accept");
        String type = "xml";
        if (acceptHeader == null || acceptHeader.isEmpty() ||
            acceptHeader.equals("application/xml")) {
            representation = MessageBO.getXML(messageID);
        } else if (acceptHeader.equals("application/json")) {
            representation = MessageBO.getJSON(messageID);
            type = "json";
        }

        return new DefaultHttpHeaders(type).disableCaching();
    }

    // POST /messages
    public HttpHeaders create() {
        try {
```

```
            representation = MessageBO.create(CommonUtil
                .convertInputStreamToString(request
                    .getInputStream())) ;
        } catch (InvalidXMLException e) {
            throw new RuntimeException("Invalid XML.");
        } catch (UserNotFoundException e) {
            throw new RuntimeException("User not found.");
        } catch (IOException e) {
            throw new RuntimeException("Error reading input
                stream.");

        }

        return new DefaultHttpHeaders("xml").disableCaching();
    }

    // DELETE /messages/{messageID}
    public HttpHeaders destroy() {
        try {
            MessageBO.delete(messageID);
        } catch (ItemNotFoundException e) {
            throw new RuntimeException("Username not found.");
        }

        return null;
    }

    public String getRepresentation() {
        return representation;
    }

    public Object getModel() {
        return representation;
    }

    public void setId(String id) {
        this.messageID = id;
    }

    public void setServletRequest(HttpServletRequest request) {
        this.request = request;
    }
}
```

This class follows the same coding pattern we described for the `UsersController`
class, with two minor differences: first, we use the `MessageBO` helper class; and,
second, we don't allow message updates (we have no PUT request handler, so no
`update()` method).

/usermessages/{username}

The full listing for the `UsermessagesController` class, which retrieves messages stored by a particular user, looks as follows:

```java
package web;

import javax.servlet.http.HttpServletRequest;
import org.apache.struts2.convention.annotation.Result;
import org.apache.struts2.convention.annotation.Results;
import org.apache.struts2.interceptor.ServletRequestAware;
import org.apache.struts2.rest.DefaultHttpHeaders;
import org.apache.struts2.rest.HttpHeaders;
import business.MessageBO;
import com.opensymphony.xwork2.ModelDriven;

@Results( { @Result(name = "success", type = "redirectAction") })
public class UsermessagesController implements ModelDriven<Object>,
ServletRequestAware {
    private String username;
    private String representation;
    private HttpServletRequest request;

    // GET /usermessages/{username}
    public HttpHeaders show() {
        String acceptHeader = request.getHeader("Accept");
        String type = "xml";
        if (acceptHeader == null || acceptHeader.isEmpty() ||
            acceptHeader.equals("application/xml")) {
            representation = MessageBO.getAllXMLForUser(username);
        } else if (acceptHeader.equals("application/json")) {
            representation = MessageBO.getAllJSONForUser(username);
            type = "json";
        }
        return new DefaultHttpHeaders(type).disableCaching();
    }

    public String getRepresentation() {
        return representation;
    }

    public Object getModel() {
        return representation;
    }

    public void setId(String id) {
        this.username = id;
    }
```

```
        public void setServletRequest(HttpServletRequest request) {
            this.request = request;
        }
    }
```

In this action class we only support GET requests and, just as we did for previously described GET requests, we use the HTTP header *Accept* to handle content negotiation. Subsequently, we search our data storage layer through a call to `MessageBO.getAllXMLForUser()` for the XML representation of all messages, or a call to `MessageBO.getAllJSONForUser()` for the JSON representation of all messages. Note that we are reusing the view files `json.jsp` and `xml.jsp`.

/searchmessages/{search_item}

The full listing of the `SearchmessagesController` class, which searches for the `String search_item` in all stored messages, looks as follows:

```
package web;

import javax.servlet.http.HttpServletRequest;
import org.apache.struts2.convention.annotation.Result;
import org.apache.struts2.convention.annotation.Results;
import org.apache.struts2.interceptor.ServletRequestAware;
import org.apache.struts2.rest.DefaultHttpHeaders;
import org.apache.struts2.rest.HttpHeaders;
import business.MessageBO;
import com.opensymphony.xwork2.ModelDriven;

@Results( { @Result(name = "success", type = "redirectAction") })
public class SearchmessagesController implements ModelDriven<Object>,
    ServletRequestAware {
    private String search_item;
    private String representation;
    private HttpServletRequest request;

    // GET /searchmessages/{search_item}
    public HttpHeaders show() {
        String acceptHeader = request.getHeader("Accept");
        String type = "xml";
        if (acceptHeader == null || acceptHeader.isEmpty()
            || acceptHeader.equals("application/xml")) {
            representation = MessageBO.searchAllXML(search_item);
        } else if (acceptHeader.equals("application/json")) {
            representation = MessageBO.searchAllJSON(search_item);
            type = "json";
        }
```

```
            return new DefaultHttpHeaders(type).disableCaching();
    }
    public String getRepresentation() {
        return representation;
    }
    public Object getModel() {
        return representation;
    }
    public void setId(String id) {
        this.search_item = id;
    }
    public void setServletRequest(HttpServletRequest request) {
        this.request = request;
    }
}
```

This class looks like the one we coded to retrieve messages for a particular user, except that we now use different business layer calls: MessageBO.searchAllXML() for an XML representation and MessageBO.searchAllJSON() for a JSON representation.

Summary

In this chapter, we learned how to fully code a RESTful web service using the Struts 2 framework and the REST plugin. Because the plugin is a work in progress, we had to tweak some portions of the implementation to properly handle content negotiation using the HTTP *Accept* header, and also to parse the payload of POST and PUT requests. Even though the REST plugin offers automatic URI parsing and automatic content negotiation using URIs, understanding how to extend the framework to create web services that adhere to the REST constraints, as outlined by Fielding's dissertation, opens the framework to a wider audience, because it doesn't depend on the web browser being the only client.

And with this chapter, we end our exploration of the most popular open source RESTful Java frameworks available today. However, we still have a few topics to cover in the remainder of the book. In the next two chapters, we'll study more RESTful clients and standalone servers using the Restlet libraries, and we'll look at performance and security issues revolving around RESTful web services.

9
Restlet Clients and Servers

In this chapter, we cover the parts of the Restlet framework that we didn't cover in Chapter 6, *The Restlet Framework*, because we specifically deployed our web service in a Java web container. However, the Restlet framework provides libraries to create standalone applications, including RESTful clients and RESTful servers.

At the end of this chapter, you'll be able to create Restlet clients and create and deploy RESTful web services that run as standalone Java applications that don't require a full-blown Java web server.

Getting the tools

If you have downloaded and unpacked the tools we used in Chapter 6, you already have everything we need here. Nevertheless, the list of tools is as follows:

Software	Web location
Java JDK	`http://java.sun.com/`
Db4o	`http://developer.db4o.com/files/default.aspx`
Restlet Framework 2.0	`http://www.restlet.org/downloads/`

Download and install the latest JDK; also download and unpack Db4o and the Restlet framework, noting their unpacked location, as we need a few libraries to compile and run the applications we code.

All the source code listed in this chapter is available from `http://www.packtpub.com/files/code/6460_Code.zip` (look for `Chapter9`). You can download the source package to follow along the code samples, or, in some cases, you can just type the full examples presented here and then compile and run them.

Restlet standalone applications

In Chapter 6, we studied the Servlet integration portion of the Restlet framework. In this chapter, we look at two other aspects of the framework, namely, the client facility and the standalone server facility.

Restlet clients

In Chapters 2 and 3, *Accessing RESTful Services – Part 1* and *2*, we covered different client types to connect to RESTful web services. However, the Restlet framework offers another option and provides libraries to handle HTTP connections, which are abstracted at a higher level from the Java net packages or the Commons HTTP Client library.

HTTP GET requests

A standalone client consuming responses from HTTP requests to web services, using the Restlet framework, looks as follows:

```
import java.io.IOException;
import org.restlet.resource.ClientResource;
import org.restlet.resource.ResourceException;
public class StandAloneClient {
    public static void main(String[] args) {
        try {
            new ClientResource("http://www.google.com/")
                .get().write(System.out);
        } catch (IOException e) {
            e.printStackTrace();
        } catch (ResourceException e) {
            e.printStackTrace();
        }
    }
}
```

In this example we connect to `http://www.google.com/` and display the result to the standard out stream. A run of this application looks as follows:

```
Jul 16, 2009 10:48:27 AM org.restlet.engine.http.StreamClientHelper start
INFO: Starting the HTTP client
<!doctype html><html><head><meta http-equiv="content-type" content="text/
html; charset=ISO-8859-1"><title>Google</title>...[THE REST OF THE
RESPONSE IS OMMITED]
```

The result of this call is a straight read of the HTTP response, which returns an HTML document beginning with `<!doctype html>`.

We begin to see similarities with the standard Java network package, where we connect to a URL and consume the result. However, the `org.restlet.resource.ClientResource` class offers a more structured facility to connect to RESTful web services than any of the other client examples we already studied. Specifically, we can use the `get()` method of the class to negotiate resource representations by providing a `org.restlet.data.MediaType` parameter at calling time. For instance, if we wanted an XML representation from a specific URI, we would use the `get()` method like this: `get(org.restlet.data.MediaType.APPLICATION_XML)`. In code, if we were connecting to the web service we coded in Chapter 6 and we wanted a list of users in an XML format, the request would look as follows:

```
ClientResource("http://localhost:8080/RESTfulJava_Chapter5/users")
    .get(MediaType.APPLICATION_XML);
```

The Restlet client library also has methods for the other HTTP requests we've covered (POST, PUT, and DELETE).

HTTP POST requests

A standalone client making POST requests to a web service looks as follows:

```
import org.restlet.data.MediaType;
import org.restlet.representation.Representation;
import org.restlet.representation.StringRepresentation;
import org.restlet.resource.ClientResource;
import org.restlet.resource.ResourceException;

public class StandAloneClientPOST {

    public static void main(String[] args) {
        try {
            // Build a representation
            StringBuilder xml = new StringBuilder();
            xml.append("<user>").append("\n");
            xml.append("<username>restful</username>")
            xml.append("\n");
            xml.append("<password>restful</password>")
            xml.append("\n");
            xml.append("</user>");

            Representation representation =
                new StringRepresentation(xml.toString(),
                    MediaType.APPLICATION_XML);

            // POST the representation
```

```
            new ClientResource("http://localhost:8080
                /RESTfulJava_Chapter5/users")
                    .post(representation);
        } catch (ResourceException e) {
            e.printStackTrace();
        }
    }
}
```

The execution of a POST request is similar to a GET request, except that we use the `post()` method and an `org.restlet.representation.StringRepresenation` object as the parameter of the request.

For this example, we use the web service we coded in Chapter 5, *Jersey: JAX-RS*, and we use the URI for /users. If we recall, a POST request to this URI accepts an XML representation and creates the resource if it doesn't exist.

Before we run the client application, the list looks as follows:

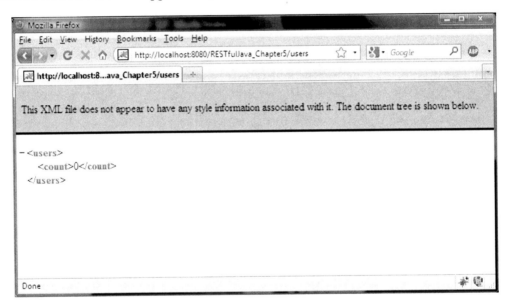

After we run the Restlet client, our resources list looks as follows:

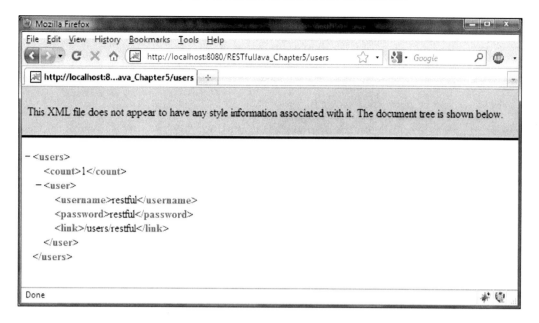

HTTP PUT requests

A standalone client making PUT requests to a web service looks as follows:

```
import org.restlet.data.MediaType;
import org.restlet.representation.Representation;
import org.restlet.representation.StringRepresentation;
import org.restlet.resource.ClientResource;
import org.restlet.resource.ResourceException;

public class StandAloneClientPUT {

    public static void main(String[] args) {
        try {
            // Build a representation
            StringBuilder xml = new StringBuilder();
            xml.append("<user>").append("\n");
            xml.append("<username>restful</username>").append("\n");
            xml.append("<password>restful2</password>").append("\n");
            xml.append("</user>");

            Representation representation = new
                StringRepresentation(xml.toString(),
                    MediaType.APPLICATION_XML);

            // PUT the representation
```

```
              new ClientResource("http://localhost:8080
                 /RESTfulJava_Chapter5/users/restful")
                      .put(representation);
          } catch (ResourceException e) {
              e.printStackTrace();
          }
      }
  }
```

This application is similar to the application executing POST requests, except that we use the put() method. The representation is identical to the one we used previously, though the URI is now of the form /users/restful, restful being the resource we want to update.

After running the application, the list of users now looks as follows (note the password field updated):

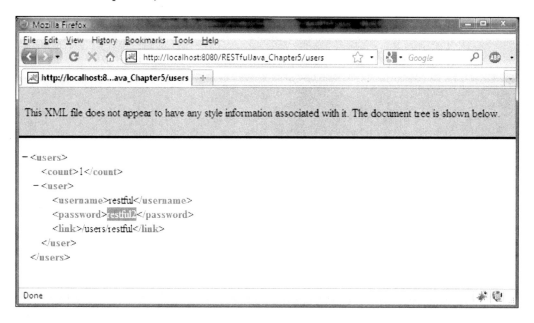

HTTP DELETE requests

A standalone client making DELETE requests to a web service looks as follows:

```
import org.restlet.resource.ClientResource;
import org.restlet.resource.ResourceException;

public class StandAloneClientDELETE {

    public static void main(String[] args) {
```

```
        try {
            new ClientResource("http://localhost:8080
                /RESTfulJava_Chapter5/users/restful").delete();
        } catch (ResourceException e) {
            e.printStackTrace();
        }
    }
}
```

Again, the coding pattern is similar to the other request types, except that we use the `delete()` method, though the URI remains the same (`/users/restful`).

If we run this application immediately after the last one, the list of users now looks as follows:

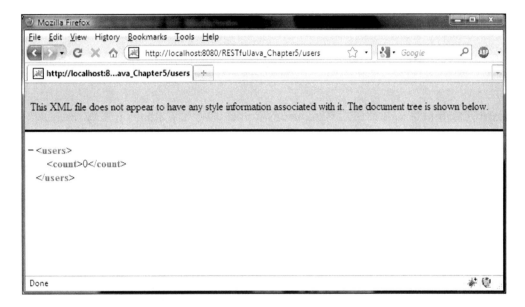

Restlet servers

The Restlet framework also includes a light version of an HTTP server that listens to a TCP/IP port just like a full Java web container does. A Restlet server requires minimum installation and is configuration- and maintenance-free: a Restlet server just runs, which makes it very convenient when minimum server tinkering is the goal.

We can create a Restlet server out of any `org.restlet.resource.ServerResource` class by attaching it to a `org.restlet.Server` instance (together with a free port) in a class's `main()` method. Assuming that port 8006 is available in our local machine, we create a standalone RESTful web service as follows:

```
import org.restlet.Server;
import org.restlet.data.Protocol;
import org.restlet.resource.Get;
import org.restlet.resource.ServerResource;

public class StandAloneServer extends ServerResource {
    public static void main(String[] args) throws Exception {
        new Server(Protocol.HTTP, 8006, StandAloneServer.class)
            .start();
    }

    @Get
    public String toString() {
        return "RESTful Java Web Services with Restlet.";
    }
}
```

This application listens to HTTP requests on port 8006. We attach an `org.restlet.resource.ServerResource` and start a server thread as follows:

```
new Server(Protocol.HTTP, 8006, StandAloneServer.class).start();
```

The Restlet framework provides all the piping required for this application to run, without the heavy duty stack of a full Java web container such as Tomcat or JBoss. (Although, technically the server is Java web server that requires no installation or maintenance, but only handles RESTful calls.)

In this example, we only support the GET request through the `@Get` annotated method `toString()`, which returns a String object to the calling client (remember that the name of the annotated method is arbitrary). With the server started, we can now make a request to the URI `http://localhost:8006/` that looks as follows:

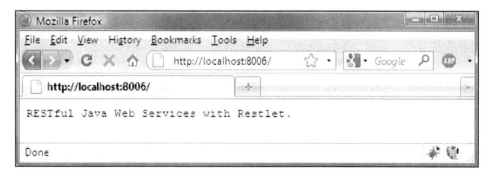

A web browser, by default, sends HTTP GET requests through the address bar; therefore, our request is handled by the annotated `toString()` method and sends the String object we defined in the previous code listing. Subsequently, any GET request to our Restlet server on port 8006 gets handled by the same annotated method. For example, a request to `http://localhost:8006/temp/temp` will also output the same string message, like this:

We can make our standalone server POST-aware by adding an annotated `@Post` method. The modified application looks as follows:

```
import org.restlet.Server;
import org.restlet.data.Protocol;
import org.restlet.resource.Get;
import org.restlet.resource.Post;
import org.restlet.resource.ServerResource;
public class StandAloneServer extends ServerResource {
    public static void main(String[] args) throws Exception {
        new Server(Protocol.HTTP, 8006, StandAloneServer.class)
            .start();
    }
    @Get
    public String toString() {
        return "RESTful Java Web Services with Restlet.";
    }
    @Post
    public String handlePost() {
        return "HTTP POST - RESTful Java Web Services with Restlet.";
    }
}
```

Connecting to our standalone server to execute the POST request takes nothing more than sending an HTTP request with any client that can generate POST messages. To test our POST handling method, we can use the Java Swing application we coded in Chapter 2, *Accessing RESTful Services – Part 1*, as follows:

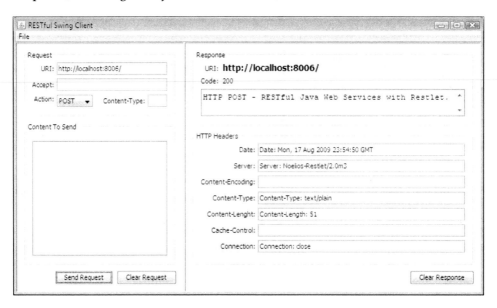

Note the **Response** in the right pane of the Swing application. Also, note that if we change the **Action** type to a **GET** from a **POST**, we get the following response:

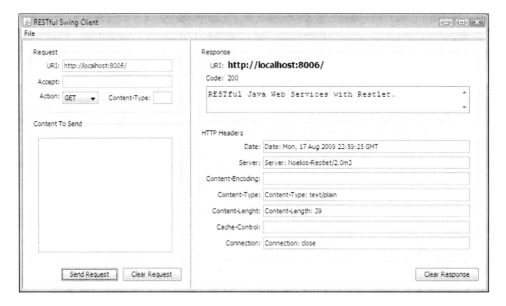

The **Response** pane displays what we expect: the string result from our `@Get` annotated method.

Finally, we can make our standalone server handle PUT and DELETE HTTP requests by adding the two respective annotated methods. The full listing for a complete RESTful web service that handles full resource CRUD-like actions looks as follows:

```java
import org.restlet.Server;
import org.restlet.data.Protocol;
import org.restlet.resource.Delete;
import org.restlet.resource.Get;
import org.restlet.resource.Post;
import org.restlet.resource.Put;
import org.restlet.resource.ServerResource;
public class StandAloneServer extends ServerResource {
    public static void main(String[] args) throws Exception {
        new Server(Protocol.HTTP, 8006, StandAloneServer.class)
            .start();
    }

    @Get
    public String toString() {
        return "HTTP GET - RESTful Java Web Services with Restlet.";
    }

    @Post
    public String handlePost() {
        return "HTTP POST - RESTful Java Web Services with Restlet.";
    }

    @Put
    public String handlePut() {
        return "HTTP PUT - RESTful Java Web Services with Restlet.";
    }

    @Delete
    public String handleDelete() {
        return "HTTP DELETE - RESTful Java Web Services with
            Restlet.";
    }
}
```

Again, to test our standalone web service, we use the Java Swing client to send PUT and DELETE requests. The **PUT** request, together with its **Response**, looks as follows:

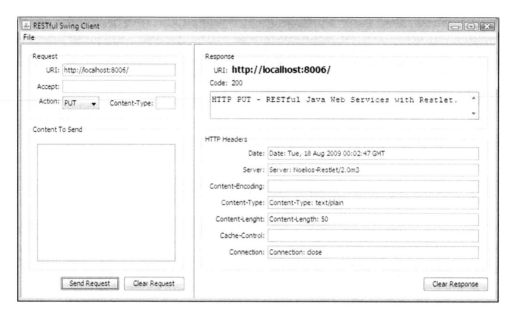

And the **DELETE** request, together with its **Response**, looks as follows:

This server only returns a generic string representation to every request. However, we can modify the request handlers to parse URIs that could include parameters, and also to send back proper resource representations of whatever our problem domain requires. What's more, because the server is a Restlet resource, the code explanations from Chapter 6, *The Restlet Framework*, apply here as well.

Take for instance the resource class we coded in Chapter 6 to handle GET and POST requests related to users (the URI /users), where a GET request returns a representation of all users in the database and a POST request creates a new user in the database. We can create the same functionality of the Java container web service of Chapter 6 as a standalone web service.

Assume that the main requirement to develop a standalone RESTful web service — a desktop application that can't run inside a Java web container such as Tomcat. As per the examples we just saw, we can simply add a `main()` method to the Restlet resource class and then execute it as a Java application. The full RESTful web service to handle GET and POST requests for the URI /users looks as follows:

```java
import java.io.IOException;

import org.restlet.Server;
import org.restlet.data.MediaType;
import org.restlet.data.Protocol;
import org.restlet.data.Status;
import org.restlet.representation.Representation;
import org.restlet.representation.StringRepresentation;
import org.restlet.resource.Get;
import org.restlet.resource.Post;
import org.restlet.resource.ServerResource;

import exception.InvalidXMLException;
import exception.ItemAlreadyExistsException;

import business.UserBO;

public class UsersResourceStandalone extends ServerResource {
    public static void main(String[] args) throws Exception {
        new Server(Protocol.HTTP, 8007,
            UsersResourceStandalone.class).start();
    }

    @Get("xml")
    public Representation getXML() {
        String xml = UserBO.getAllXML();
        Representation representation = new
            StringRepresentation(xml, MediaType.APPLICATION_XML);
        return representation;
    }
```

```
@Post
public Representation createtUser(Representation entity) {
    Representation representation = null;

    try {
        representation = new StringRepresentation
            (UserBO.create(entity.getText()),
                MediaType.APPLICATION_XML);
    } catch (InvalidXMLException e) {
        setStatus(Status.CLIENT_ERROR_BAD_REQUEST);
        representation = new StringRepresentation("Invalid XML.",
            MediaType.TEXT_PLAIN);
    } catch (ItemAlreadyExistsException e) {
        setStatus(Status.CLIENT_ERROR_FORBIDDEN);
        representation = new StringRepresentation("Item already
            exists.", MediaType.TEXT_PLAIN);
    } catch (IOException e) {
        setStatus(Status.SERVER_ERROR_INTERNAL );
    }

    return representation;
}
}
```

Nothing has changed from the code we saw in Chapter 6, except that we now have added a `main()` method as follows:

```
public static void main(String[] args) throws Exception {
    new Server(Protocol.HTTP, 8007, UsersResourceStandalone.class)
        .start();
}
```

By using this coding pattern, we don't run our Restlet resource within the confines of a Java web container. This means that we have no XML deployment configuration or web server installation and maintenance.

With this standalone web service, we can now manage user representations through the URI `http://localhost:8007/`. (Note that the full listing of the application `UsersResourceStandalone` uses the *business* layer package we used in previous chapters to delegate resource serialization—this was already explained, and the full code listing is part of the chapter's source package.)

Assuming our application is running in our local machine and that the TCP/IP port 8007 is available, we make GET requests — using Firefox — as follows:

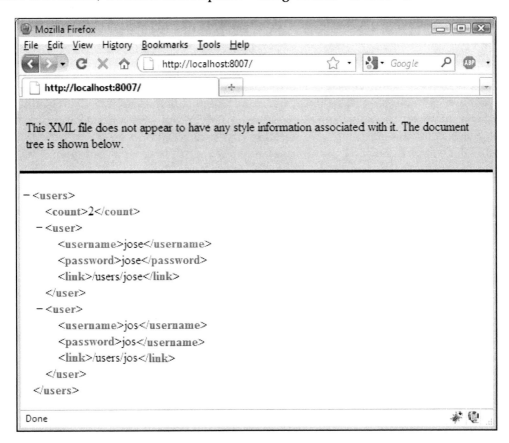

This is, unsurprisingly, the same result we get by using the URI pointing to the web service from Chapter 6. The difference here is that we are running a standalone Java application and not using a Java web container.

We can extend this approach further and create RESTful web services that run from multiple machines that don't require a full Java web container running at all times. What's more, this approach offers granular control of what can be made available as a RESTful web service on a per TCP/IP port basis. For example, a specific port serving GET requests or POST requests.

Finally, compiling and running the applications in this chapter only require that we add the proper JAR files for the `javac` and `java` commands. Specifically, we need the files `org.restlet.jar` and `db4o-7.4.88.12908-java5.jar`.

Summary

In this chapter, we covered the last two main offerings of the Restlet framework that were not covered in Chapter 6. Even though we already studied different ways to connect to RESTful web services, the Restlet client library offers an annotated solution that mirrors a RESTful web service implementation.

The more valuable of these last two topics, however, is the Restlet server library. Sometimes we're faced with restrictions from IT departments where we can't fully deploy a Java web container, but we require a full RESTful web service running on a particular machine. Without a lightweight and configuration-free server offered by the Restlet server library, we would need to embed a full Java web container in our applications, thus increasing the complexity of our code base.

10

Security and Performance

In this chapter, we take the point of view of the architect and not of the creator of the infrastructures supporting our applications. Nevertheless, at the end of the chapter, you'll have a thorough understanding of how to secure your web services using HTTP basic authentication, and a thorough understanding of when and how to use the OAuth authentication protocol. Furthermore, you'll gain a working knowledge of scalability and availability and how these two combine to create high performing web services.

Security

Security on the Internet takes many forms. In the context of RESTful web services and this book, we're only interested in two forms of security: first, *securing* access to web services; second, *accessing* web services on behalf of our users.

Securing web services

What we accomplish with securing web services is calculated control of resources. Even though most web services are publicly available, we still need to control data access and traffic throughput. We can do both by restricting access through subscription accounts. For example, Google's web service API (now defunct), limited the number of queries a registered user could execute daily. Similarly, the semantic mashup we coded in Chapter 3, *Accessing RESTful Services — Part 2*, has a limited number of semantic parsing requests per day.

In this section, we cover two of the most popular options: custom token authentication and HTTP basic authentication.

Custom token authentication

Custom token authentication is likely the easiest authentication method to implement. The process entails two steps: first, generating a unique token per registered API user; second, each registered user sends the generated token for authentication with every request to the service. Because we send a token with every request, this method is not secure, as someone can copy a valid token and use it without authorization. What's more, we have no way of telling if the request is legitimate or not.

Generating an access token is independent of the web service and is as simple as creating a user registration process that generates a unique token per account. Access is then controlled on a per request basis, because every data exchange can be logged and verified.

The authentication token is sent with every request in two ways: it can be part of the URI, or it can be added to the HTTP request header.

We look in detail at the URI solution. An example of this method is Yahoo's Search API, which uses the following URI format:

```
http://search.yahooapis.com/WebSearchService/V1/webSearch?appid=YahooD
emo&query=finances&format=pdf
```

The token in this URI is the value for `appid`, which is `YahooDemo`. If we had a registered account to use this API, we would have a unique token to pass for every request.

If we wanted to add this authentication method for our sample web service (the one we implemented using the four frameworks we covered), every URI would require a token that should have been created before using the service. For instance, our now-familiar URI to request all users from our database layer would look like `/users/token={UNIQUE_TOKEN}`.

Parsing the token at the framework level is trivial, as we already know how to consume dynamic variables in URIs. Our full API, together with custom token authentication, would look as follows:

URI with unique token
`http://localhost:8080/users/token={token}`
`http://localhost:8080/users/{username}/token={token}`
`http://localhost:8080/messages/token={token}`
`http://localhost:8080/messages/{messageID}/token={token}`
`http://localhost:8080/messages/users/{username}/token={token}`
`http://localhost:8080/messages/search/{search_item}/token={token}`

Parsing this new variable using the Jersey (or RESTEasy) framework is a matter of properly defining the URI in the resource class and consuming the value in each annotated method. For instance, the resource `UsersResource` class, which handles GET requests and returns a list of users, would look as follows:

```
@Path("/users/token={token}")
public class UsersResource {
    @GET
    @Produces("application/xml")
    public String getXML(@PathParam("token") String token) {
        if (AuthenticationService.authenticate(token)) {
            return UserBO.getAllXML();
        } else {
            throw new WebApplicationException(401);
        }
    }
}
```

This class handles only GET requests and returns a list of users in the system as an XML representation. This is the same code we saw in Chapter 5, *Jersey: JAX-RS*, with the exception that we have introduced the authentication step. The representation is served if and only if the token passed in the URI is validated by our authentication process with `AuthenticationService.authenticate(token)`. Note that the call to the `AuthenticationService` class is only an example of where the authentication would need to take place—this class is not part of the source code. Finally, if a request is made with an invalid token, we throw a web exception with the status code 401, which is the standard numeric code for unauthorized access.

To summarize, using our API would now require users to first create an account, which in turn would generate a unique token, and, finally, each request to our web service would require the generated token to be sent in the URI and validated for each request. With this scheme in place, we now have control of disabling a user's token depending on whatever rules we have defined in our terms of service contract. For example, if a limit on the number of requests per day has been reached, we can turn off access automatically.

The URI convention to pass the token is arbitrary, and we could, for example, prefer the URI /users/token:{UNIQUE_TOKEN} over the URI /users/token={UNIQUE_TOKEN}.

HTTP basic authentication

Basic HTTP authentication works by sending the cleartext, Base64 encoded username and password pair in the HTTP header *Authorization*. The username and password must be sent for every HTTP request for the authorization to be validated. A typical HTTP basic authentication transaction can be depicted with the following sequence diagram, where we request an XML representation of users to the URI /users:

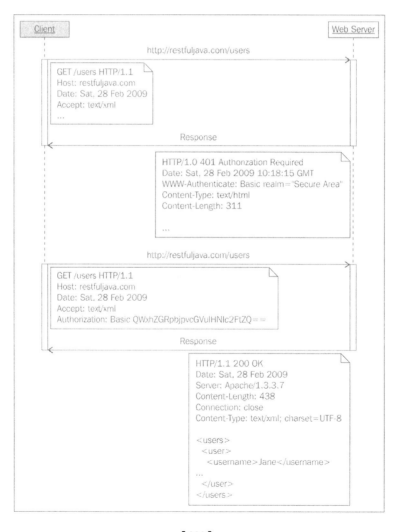

This diagram represents a whole transaction. A client begins by requesting the URI `/users`. Because the resource is secured using HTTP basic authentication and the client doesn't provide the required authorization credentials, the server replies with a 401 HTTP response. The client receives the response and takes action by setting the appropriate credentials and sends back a new request to the same URI. This time the server verifies the credentials and replies back with the requested resource.

As we've seen, client requests can be generated from any application that can create HTTP connections, including web browsers. Web browsers, typically, cache the credentials so that users don't have to type in their username and password for every secured resource request. If credentials are cached, the client using them can't logout as we think of the logout action — this is viewed as deficiency of the protocol, as unauthorized access can take place with cache credentials, and there is no way for a web service to differentiate from authorized or unauthorized. Furthermore, using basic authentication is not secure because usernames and passwords are only encoded using Base64 encoding, which can be easily deciphered. However, the intent of Base64 is not to secure the name/value pair, but to uniformly encode characters when transferred over HTTP. In general, we solve this potential security hole by using HTTPS (SSL) instead of HTTP.

Clients and basic authentication

A normal client/server transaction, when using HTTP basic authentication, can take two forms. On the one hand, a client makes a request to the server without authentication credentials (as depicted in the last sequence diagram). On the other hand, a client makes a request to the server with authentication credentials.

First, when a client makes a request without authentication credentials, the server sends a response with an HTTP error code of 401 (unauthorized access). If the request is executed from a web browser, users see the ubiquitous **Authentication Required** browser popup that looks as follows (we are accessing a resource from `http://sandoval.ca/`):

Users can now enter a valid username and password to complete the request. Note that the web browser keeps track of the 401 response and is charged with sending the proper authentication credentials back with the original URI—this makes the transaction seamless for users. Now, if we were using a client other than a web browser, we would need to programmatically intercept the 401 response and then provide valid credentials to complete the original request.

The second scenario that comes up using HTTP basic authentication is when we don't wait for a server's 401 response, but provide authentication credentials from the beginning. As we said, we provide the credentials in the HTTP header *Authorization*. Setting the HTTP headers varies from client to client, so we present how to send valid credentials using the Commons HTTP Client library. A valid request, together with valid credentials, looks as follows:

```
. . .
HttpClient client = new HttpClient();

client.getState().setCredentials(new AuthScope("www.restfuljava.com",
    443, "realm"), new UsernamePasswordCredentials("username",
        "password"));

GetMethod get = new GetMethod("http://www.restfuljava.com/webservice
                                                        /users");

get.setDoAuthentication(true);

client.executeMethod(get);
. . .
```

Assuming that the resource we need has the URI `http://www.restfuljava.com/webservice/users`, and the username and password are `username` and `password`, we set the credentials with the method call `setCredentials()`. We, then, instantiate a `GetMethod` object to execute with our `client` object instance. Because we are sending authentication credentials from the get go, we don't expect a 401 response from the server and the consumption of the representation requested proceeds as any other request.

For the other HTTP request types (POST, PUT, and DELETE), we would follow the same pattern: we set the credentials and proceed with the request and consumption of the response. Finally, every request type must include the authentication credentials or else we have to handle programmatically the server's 401 response.

For details of HTTP basic authentication, see
`http://www.ietf.org/rfc/rfc2617.txt`.

Servers and basic authentication

In this section, we cover how to configure our web services to challenge connecting clients for valid authentication credentials.

Basic authentication configuration depends on the web container being used. Throughout this book, we've used Tomcat for every application that required a Java web container; therefore, we only look at basic authentication configuration for the latest version of Tomcat (6.x).

The problem to solve is restricting access to our RESTful web services. Using basic authentication, we can do this in two ways: first, we have only one set of credentials that every registered user uses; second, we create a set of users for a specific realm.

Single username and password

This process is recommended when there's no limit of requests per user or we don't care that multiple users share the same username and password (in an intranet environment, for example).

Basic authentication configuration is done through the files web.xml (part of the web application, which is located in the application's WEB-INF directory) and tomcat-users.xml (part of Tomcat's configuration, which is located in Tomcat's conf directory).

Let's say we want to use basic authentication for the Jersey implementation of our sample web service (found in Chapter 5, *Jersey: JAX-RS*). We can modify the web.xml file to look as follows:

```
<?xml version="1.0" encoding="UTF-8"?>
<web-app version="2.5"
    xmlns="http://java.sun.com/xml/ns/javaee"
    xmlns:xsi="http://www.w3.org/2001/XMLSchema-instance"
    xsi:schemaLocation="http://java.sun.com/xml/ns/javaee
    http://java.sun.com/xml/ns/javaee/web-app_2_5.xsd">
    <servlet>
        <servlet-name>JerseyTest</servlet-name>
        <servlet-class>
            com.sun.jersey.spi.container.servlet.ServletContainer
        </servlet-class>
        <load-on-startup>1</load-on-startup>
    </servlet>
    <servlet-mapping>
        <servlet-name>JerseyTest</servlet-name>
        <url-pattern>/*</url-pattern>
    </servlet-mapping>
    <welcome-file-list>
        <welcome-file>index.jsp</welcome-file>
```

```
    </welcome-file-list>
    <!-- Everything below is for basic authentication -->
    <security-constraint>
        <web-resource-collection>
            <web-resource-name>
                RESTful Java Web Services
            </web-resource-name>
            <url-pattern>/*</url-pattern>
        </web-resource-collection>
        <auth-constraint>
            <role-name>user</role-name>
        </auth-constraint>
    </security-constraint>
    <!-- Login Configuration -->
    <login-config>
        <auth-method>BASIC</auth-method>
        <realm-name>RESTful Java Web Services</realm-name>
    </login-config>
</web-app>
```

The top half of this listing is the same one we used for the application's deployment in Chapter 5. The bottom half is part of our basic authentication configuration. All the XML tags are Tomcat specific, and are telling the web server that the web application containing this web.xml file uses basic authentication and that any URI access must be authenticated for role-name user. This means that access to the URI http://localhost:8080/RESTfulJava_Chapter5/users requires the username and password that is in the tomcat-users.xml.

To add a user, we modify the tomcat-users.xml file as follows:

```
<?xml version='1.0' encoding='utf-8'?>
    <tomcat-users>
        <role rolename="user"/>
        <user username="username" password="password" roles="user"/>
    </tomcat-users>
```

For this example, the username and password values are username and password, with the value for roles of user. With these two files modified, we now have a RESTful web service using basic authentication. (If you are trying this for the web service in Chapter 5, remember that you must restart the web container every time either of these two files is modified.)

As we already mentioned, the credentials for this Tomcat user are shared with every user accessing the web service. In other words, if we wanted to give access to a new user, we would just pass along the username and password in the tomcat-users.xml file.

Tomcat realms

What if we want more than one user? We can see that the approach we just discussed is not scalable, because we would need to continue adding users to the `tomcat-users.xml` file and would then need to restart the web container every time a new user is added. Therefore, Tomcat offers multiple user support for basic authentication with the concept of *realms*.

A **realm** is a database that stores usernames and passwords for multiple users. Tomcat offers various credential realms, including JDBCRealm, DataSourceRealm, JNDIRealm, MemoryRealm, and JAASRealm. We can also create a custom realm by implementing the `org.apache.catalina.Realm` interface, which is part of the installed Tomcat libraries.

Full discussion of realm configuration is already well covered in Tomcat's documentation at `http://tomcat.apache.org/tomcat-6.0-doc/realm-howto.html`; therefore, for the sake of brevity, we don't cover any of these configuration methods. Nevertheless, remember that any user registration process you choose has to be integrated with Tomcat's realm so that user creation and credentials creation are part of the same transaction. In other words, a user registering to use your RESTful web services must also be registered with the Tomcat realm you are using.

The two basic authentication methods described here have the same fundamental security hole of sending credentials as cleartext in every HTTP request. Therefore, we need a mechanism to ensure that credentials can't be spoofed during a transaction. One of the solutions to this problem — among HTTP digest authentication or custom encryption schemes such as Amazon's web service authentication — is to use the **Secure Socket Layer (SSL)** protocol.

SSL is a well understood web protocol and because the RESTful web services we implemented in previous chapters are nothing more than server components, all we need to do is configure Tomcat to use SSL; therefore, every request and response messages between clients and servers, assuming SSL has been configured properly, would now be encrypted.

Just remember that once SSL has been turned on, requests are now HTTPS requests — this means that URIs take the form of `https://localhost:8080/RESTfulJava_Chapter5/users` (note the `https` prefix in the address).

For the sake of brevity, we haven't covered how to configure SSL, though Tomcat's documentation has an excellent how-to guide at `http://tomcat.apache.org/tomcat-6.0-doc/ssl-howto.html`.

OAuth — accessing web services on behalf of users

OAuth solves a different security problem from what HTTP basic authentication has been used for—securing access to web services.

OAuth is an authorization protocol that allows third-party web service creators to get access to users' data stored in a different web service, but only with users' consent and without a username and password exchange. Specifically, authorization here means that a third-party web service (the *consumer service*) makes a request to use data stored in a different web service (the *provider service*) on behalf of a user (*Jane*). The consumer and provider services are independent from each other, and each web service has its own login information.

Before OAuth—or other similar open source protocols such as Google AuthSub and FlickrAuth—if Jane wanted the consumer service using her data on the provider service, she needed to give her provider's credentials to the consumer service.

Instead of Jane passing her login information to multiple third party services, OAuth solves this problem by letting the consumer service request authorization from the provider service on Jane's behalf. Jane doesn't divulge her login information: authorization is granted from the provider service, where both her data and credentials are stored. The consumer service only receives an authorization token that is used to access data from the provider service. Note that the user (Jane) has full control on the transaction and can invalidate the authorization token at any time during the signup process or even after the two services have been used together.

The typical example used to explain OAuth is that of a service provider that stores pictures on the Web (let's call the service StorageInc), and a fictional consumer service that is a picture printing service (let's call the service PrintInc). On its own, PrintInc is a full-blown web service, but it doesn't offer picture storage—its business is only printing pictures. For convenience, PrintInc has created a web service that lets its users download their pictures from StorageInc for printing.

This is what happens when Jane decides to use PrintInc to print her images stored at StorageInc:

- Jane creates an account in PrintInc.

- PrintInc asks if Jane wants to use her pictures stored in StorageInc and presents a link to get authorization to download her pictures.

- Jane decides to let PrintInc connect to StorageInc on her behalf and clicks the authorization link.

- Both PrintInc and StorageInc have implemented the OAuth protocol, so StorageInc asks Jane if she wants to let PrintInc use her pictures.

  Before the authorization token is created, Jane must provide her username and password. Note, however, that her credentials are being used at StorageInc's site, and that PrintInc has no knowledge of her credentials.

- Once Jane provides her credentials, StorageInc passes PrintInc an authorization token, which is stored as part of Jane's account at PrintInc.

- Now we're back at PrintInc's web application and Jane can now print any of her pictures stored in StorageInc's web service.

- Finally, every time Jane wants to print more pictures, all she needs to do is come back to PrintInc's website and download her pictures from StorageInc. Note that she doesn't need to provide her username and password again, as she has already authorized these two web services to exchange data on her behalf.

OAuth's authorization protocol is becoming the preferred authorization scheme for service providers and service consumers, because of its simplicity and ease of integration to RESTful web services. What's more, OAuth is an open source protocol, and code samples for configuring the service provider and service consumer are readily available. Therefore, we don't cover full integration of our sample web service, but we point you to get more information from OAuth's website at `http://oauth.net/`.

If you are beginning to look into OAuth, you'll find comparisons of it to OpenID. These two technologies are different: OpenID is one of the single sign-on schemes available on the Web, where users use the same identification credentials across different web applications. Usernames and passwords are stored separately from the web application that users log into.

OAuth, as we've seen, is used to allow third-party access to data stored on other web services.

Performance

Talking about performance of RESTful web service is the same as talking about performance of web architectures in general, because RESTful web services rely on existing web technologies. Moreover, the term *performance* means different things to different people. To end users, high performance means that when they click on a link, or click on a buy button on an e-store, they get immediate results; to us developers, it means solving the typical problem of service availability and supporting architectures that are scalable.

Web services come in different shapes and sizes. Therefore, our requirements dictate how robust the supporting hardware and software architectures need to be. Some of our solutions require only one server, where everything, including the web container and database server, lives in the same box; on the other hand, other solutions require a more robust environment, where service failures are unacceptable, and therefore, a hierarchy of redundant web containers and database servers is the norm.

Our role as web service architects or developers is sometimes limited, because we don't dictate server architectures that deal with high availability and scalability. Therefore, the approach we take in this section is not of a system engineer or administrator but of a pragmatic developer, and we limit our discussion to high-level explanations and leave the implementation details to other sources. In other words, we still need to know enough about the two big terms (availability and scalability), though, most likely, we won't build the running environments from scratch—sometimes, they are just there.

High availability

High availability means zero to minimum operational downtime. Achieving zero downtime is impossible with our highly complex web architectures. Whether we like it or not, we need to bring down entire systems for maintenance, and we acknowledge that downtime is a fact of the lifecycle of web services.

How do we achieve minimum downtime? In general, high availability is achieved through hardware redundancy: if a machine fails, or is taken down for maintenance, another one takes over the work.

Designing highly available architecture is a specialized field and requires the understanding of not only web server architectures but also of database systems. Again, the main solution to this problem is redundancy, because it removes single points of failure. Following is a typical architecture of a highly redundant setup (diagram taken from *Scalable Internet Architectures*, p. 48, by Theo Schlssnagle, *Sams Publishing*):

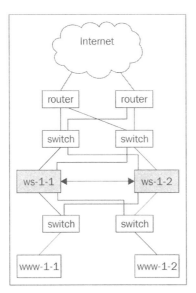

In this architecture, we have no single point of failure: if one server fails or needs to be taken down, we are guaranteed service availability, provided that the whole data center doesn't die. Of course, this design increases cost and maintenance complexity; however, there are vendors who specialize in installing and maintaining these kinds of systems.

Scalability

Scalability, in the context of the Web, means to consistently provide service regardless of the increase or decrease of web users.

Are we talking about performance? Indirectly, because a poorly performing web server can scale properly and request/response transactions take the same amount of time it takes for one user as it takes for one thousand concurrent users. In general, a scalable architecture properly manages spikes and roughs in traffic, and can shrink and grow as needed.

Scalability is accomplished through an increase or decrease of hardware. Consequently, software also plays a role in the management of these setups. Without going into details, systems can scale horizontally or vertically. For an example, let's limit our scaling problem to only the web container component, though every running logical server can be scaled. Then, horizontal scaling entails increasing the number of web servers; and vertical, increasing the number of web containers within a specific machine or machines. Implementing a highly scalable system falls under the same umbrella of the architecture we described for high availability, as the goal is the same — uninterrupted, high performing web services. Therefore, this is all that we'll say about this topic.

> Often, the terms scalability, availability, and load balancing are interchanged to mean the same thing, though they solve different problems. Nonetheless, load balancing — dealing with efficiently distributing workload from a common pool of resources — is used to build highly available and easily scalable web architectures.

On-demand infrastructures

On-demand infrastructure is sometimes called **cloud computing**. Though the term cloud computing can take multiple meanings, depending on whom you ask, the most common definition refers to on-demand scalable and highly-available computing services. This means that we can buy on-demand computing resources without worrying about setup or maintenance cost, because everything is already provided by the cloud's vendor (including hardware, networking, and software systems such as firewalls and cache facilities).

At the time of this writing, two major vendors offer cloud computing: Google and Amazon. Google offers its Google App Engine service, where developers upload web applications into a computing cloud and pay only for the resources used. And Amazon offers its Amazon Elastic Compute Cloud service (known as Amazon EC2), where developers can configure dedicated virtual servers inside Amazon's computing farm.

Although Google and Amazon offer similar services, the underlying architectures and business models are quite different. On the one hand, by using Google App Engine, developers lock themselves to only one vendor, because Google doesn't offer installation of third party software servers and application development is coupled to its distributed data storage service. Currently, Google only offers Python and Java architectures, with one database option — Google's non-relational data storage service.

On the other hand, Amazon gives developers full control of their environment, because it offers fully virtualized server technology—this makes migration of deployed web applications to a different environment easier.

 For more information on Google App Engine, visit http://code.google.com/appengine/.

For more information on Amazon EC2, visit http://aws.amazon.com/ec2/.

Performance recommendations

Getting every ounce of performance out of our web services is not only a matter of hardware optimization, but also a matter of proper software engineering. In other words, a badly designed application will perform poorly regardless of the hardware backing it up.

Whether our applications run on an in-house managed data center or on a third party computing farm, we should keep in mind the following recommendations:

- Don't optimize prematurely. This means that we should make sure everything works first, optimize server setups second, then, and only then, go back to the code to optimize our algorithms. However, we should code with performance in mind—avoid String objects concatenation, close all database connections, prefer buffered streams.

- Public web services attract a lot of traffic from third party application creators; therefore, it's a good idea to separate web traffic from API traffic. Consequently, opt to have your APIs running on dedicated servers. And remember that you can treat your own website as a consumer of your own API.

- RESTful web services are stateless: keep them that way, and you'll be able to grow horizontally (add more servers to your data center). On the other hand, if you are using a third party computing farm, this is not a concern.

- Opt, *where appropriate*, for fine-grained resource representations. In some cases, resource representations are too heavy for the problem you are solving. Ask yourself if you really need the full representation. If you don't, let your resource model guide you and request only the fields you need. For instance, in the sample web service we've used throughout this book, if we only need the password for a user, we should be able to handle URI requests of type /users/{username}/({field_name,...})—note that URI style is arbitrary and is only a suggestion.

- Where appropriate, allow for multiple resource manipulation in one URI. For example, using our sample web service, if we wanted to delete multiple users in one request, we could support the URI /users(username1,username2).

- Where appropriate, use a caching system such as memcached. Caching database results sets greatly improves application latency.

This is by no means a complete list of recommendations, but it's a good start. What's more, if you decide to host your web services on a third-party computing environment such as Google's or Amazon's, some of these recommendations would already be implemented.

Summary

In this chapter, we covered two important topics of web application development—security and performance—albeit from a higher point of view than we have done in previous chapters. Because these two topics require highly specialized knowledge, we only covered enough of them to be able to make pragmatic decision during development. In all likelihood, the supporting environments for our web services will be managed by third party vendors or internal IT departments. Nonetheless, as well rounded developers, we should understand what it takes to engineer secure, scalable, and highly-available web applications.

And with this chapter, we complete our journey of RESTful Java Web Services. We began with the theory of REST, continued with RESTful clients, dissected four Java RESTful frameworks (Jersey, Restlet, RESTEasy, and Struts 2), and completed our study with the topics of web services security and performance. The only thing left is for you to put down the book, but come back for reference as needed, begin developing your own RESTful services, and make the Web a better place.

Index

Thank you for buying
RESTful Java Web Services

Packt Open Source Project Royalties

When we sell a book written on an Open Source project, we pay a royalty directly to that project. Therefore by purchasing RESTful Java Web Services, Packt will have given some of the money received to the Java project.

In the long term, we see ourselves and you — customers and readers of our books — as part of the Open Source ecosystem, providing sustainable revenue for the projects we publish on. Our aim at Packt is to establish publishing royalties as an essential part of the service and support a business model that sustains Open Source.

If you're working with an Open Source project that you would like us to publish on, and subsequently pay royalties to, please get in touch with us.

Writing for Packt

We welcome all inquiries from people who are interested in authoring. Book proposals should be sent to author@packtpub.com. If your book idea is still at an early stage and you would like to discuss it first before writing a formal book proposal, contact us; one of our commissioning editors will get in touch with you.

We're not just looking for published authors; if you have strong technical skills but no writing experience, our experienced editors can help you develop a writing career, or simply get some additional reward for your expertise.

About Packt Publishing

Packt, pronounced 'packed', published its first book "Mastering phpMyAdmin for Effective MySQL Management" in April 2004 and subsequently continued to specialize in publishing highly focused books on specific technologies and solutions.

Our books and publications share the experiences of your fellow IT professionals in adapting and customizing today's systems, applications, and frameworks. Our solution-based books give you the knowledge and power to customize the software and technologies you're using to get the job done. Packt books are more specific and less general than the IT books you have seen in the past. Our unique business model allows us to bring you more focused information, giving you more of what you need to know, and less of what you don't.

Packt is a modern, yet unique publishing company, which focuses on producing quality, cutting-edge books for communities of developers, administrators, and newbies alike. For more information, please visit our website: www.PacktPub.com.

Java EE 5 Development with NetBeans 6

ISBN: 978-1-847195-46-3   Paperback: 400 pages

Develop professional enterprise Java EE applications quickly and easily with this popular IDE

1. Use features of the popular NetBeans IDE to improve Java EE development

2. Careful instructions and screenshots lead you through the options available

3. Covers the major Java EE APIs such as JSF, EJB 3 and JPA, and how to work with them in NetBeans

DWR Java AJAX Applications

ISBN: 978-1-847192-93-6   Paperback: 228 pages

A step-by-step example-packed guide to learning professional application development with Direct Web Remoting

1. Learn Direct Web Remoting features from scratch and how to apply DWR practically

2. Topics such as configuration, testing, and debugging are thoroughly explained through examples

3. Demonstrates advanced elements of creating user interfaces and back-end integration

Please check **www.PacktPub.com** for information on our titles

Breinigsville, PA USA
26 November 2010
249921BV00005B/8/P

9 781847 196460